# Geeks
# With
# Empathy

Jeremy Adamson

Although this publication is designed to provide accurate information in regard to the subject matter covered, the publisher and the author assume no responsibility for errors, inaccuracies, omissions, or any other inconsistencies herein. This publication is not meant as a replacement for expert assistance. If such level of assistance is required, seek the services of a professional.

Unless otherwise indicated, all characters in this book are fictitious. Any resemblance to actual persons, living or dead, is purely coincidental.

ISBN: 978-1-7383108-0-7
ASIN: B0CV7R4J8Q

Published by RJA Consulting Inc.
www.rjeremyadamson.com

# ADVANCED PRAISE

"Geeks with Empathy is a must-read for anyone in the technology sector. It's an enlightening and thought-provoking work that not only highlights the shortcomings of the current paradigm but also provides a roadmap for cultivating a more empathetic and effective approach to technology and business. Jeremy Adamson's book is a significant contribution to the conversation on the human aspects of technology and is likely to inspire meaningful change in how technology workers relate to their work, their peers, and their stakeholders."

*Achille Ettorre, Analytics Strategy Executive*

"Success in AI & analytics initiatives is fundamentally more about people than technology or algorithms. This book is a compelling guide for tech leaders seeking to elevate their teams through empathetic communication and understanding."

*Dave Keirstead, Data & Analytics Executive*

"In a world dominated by the never-ending race to the top for the best algorithms and technology comes a unique book aimed squarely at technology leaders looking to bridge the gap between machines and people. A compelling narrative on the important role empathy and communication play in driving success in the digital era. It's not about silicon and carbon. Adamson reminds us in the end that it's all about carbon-based life forms. A must read."

*Jack Phillips, CEO of the International Institute for Analytics*

"This book is a must-read for anyone who wants to succeed in the tech and data science field. It shows how empathy is not only a human virtue, but also a business advantage. It offers practical insights and strategies on how to cultivate empathy in yourself and others, and how to apply it to your work."

*Suvadip Chakraborty, Data Science Leader and Author*

**Praise for *Minding the Machines***

"For leaders craving a playbook that puts together all the key elements required for building a high performing Advanced Analytics & AI function in a comprehensive but down to earth manner, this book is most definitely a must read."

*Celia Wanderley, Chief Customer Officer at AltaML*

"... with detailed explanations and checklists throughout, anyone looking to grow an analytics and data science organization can find support within the book."

*Bill Franks, author of The Analytics Revolution, and Director, Center for Statistics and Analytical Research, Kennesaw State University*

"... a valuable resource for all parties as they advance the role of analytics, and being digital, in their organization... "

*Lee Ackerman, Digital Learning Architect, TEKsystems*

To Eleanor

Let us try in the matter of these most solemn of all interests, to look more to great truths and facts which exist quite independently of the impression they may for the time produce upon us; and less to our own fanciful or morbid frames and feelings.

*Boyd, Recreations of a County Parson (1864)*

# CONTENTS

# INTRODUCTION

*"He said you were a turnip."*

*"A turnip?"*

*"Yes, a turnip. He said I wasted 45 minutes of his time by setting up that meeting with you."*

*"He doesn't know what he's talking about - he just didn't understand how much better this approach is."*

*"I saw your deck - all you did was prove that you are better at math than he is. Was that your goal? Was that what you were hoping to get out of it? If it wasn't then you're not nearly as smart as you think you are."*

I didn't realize it at the time, but that conversation marked the most transformative moment of my career. After dedicating a year of my life to developing a new predictive model with both financial and social benefits, my mentor arranged an opportunity for me to present my findings to a senior executive within our organization. I had rehearsed and polished the presentation deck, entering the meeting with unwavering confidence. Every bullet was meticulously aligned, and every number was triple-checked.

Shortly after the presentation, I received a note requesting a visit to my mentor's office to discuss the outcome. Expecting praise for my exceptional presentation, I was caught completely off guard when I was instead labeled a turnip.

After several days of reflection, I came to acknowledge the validity of my mentor's critique. The aim of the presentation was to facilitate the implementation of the project. I needed to sell my idea to a stakeholder, but I was trying to sell it to myself.

Years later, and after countless conversations with practitioners, I've come to understand that my experience is not unique. This situation has unfolded in various forms for every technology professional, from data scientists to business analysts to software developers. Our passion for technology and our drive to employ it innovatively to enhance the organizations we serve can lead to remarkable outcomes. We create new products, streamline processes, and generate actionable insights on which organizations now rely. No aspect of modern corporate life remains untouched by the digital transformations in which we have played a role. However, the greatest challenge has never resided in data quality, tool availability, preferred technology stacks, or adopted development frameworks.

The main obstacle to unlocking real value within technology teams has been an absence of mutual understanding with the business stakeholders.

It has been a lack of empathy.

It is self-evident, but warrants being explicit: unless our work is implemented and in use, we have accomplished nothing. Perfectly conceived predictive models, unsold and unused, do nothing for the bottom line. Forgotten directories of proof-of-concept projects are not given a place on the profit and loss statement at year end.

Instead of accepting feedback from our stakeholders, we become defensive. We say that the business stakeholders did not understand the value and are impeding us once again from effecting meaningful change.

Fortunately, my mentor did not allow me to assign blame to anyone but myself for the failure to sell this new approach.

*"Start at the end - what do you want the outcome to be from this?"*

*"That's obvious, isn't it? I want our department to change the way we predict these events."*

*"Right, and he needs to approve that change. So, what's in it for him?"*

*"It's just a better way to do it - it is hundreds of times better."*

*"You're not answering the question though. What is in it for him?"*

*"The way that they do it now makes no sense. It hasn't for years. They are just using it because it is there."*

*"So what? Do you think he has ever had his hand slapped for using an established best practice? Does his boss complain that the process is not predictive enough?"*

When we purchase a product, we are seeking a solution to a very personal problem. We dislike noisy aircraft cabins, so we buy noise cancelling headphones. We want to show our pets that we love them, so we buy them treats. While our desire for products can be elicited externally, our decision to proceed always involves an evaluation, whether we are conscious of it or not, of the alternatives in light of our own value system and motivating factors. Would details on the chemistry of canine digestion entice you to buy pet treats? Would a primer on alternative ear canal gripping materials compel you to purchase earbuds? Details are a distraction from the problem that we want solved.

Telling people about a problem they didn't know they have is an awful way to convince them of something, but this is exactly our approach as technology workers. We tell our colleagues, already burdened with the daily struggles of corporate life, that we have discovered a flaw in their workflow and make demands on their time to fix it. When they challenge us, politely or otherwise, we lament our place in the cosmos, being the lone arbiter of logic, hamstrung by our ignorant colleagues.

Though often we entered technical fields because we love technology for its own sake, it is only the productive application of technology that creates value for others. We leverage our passion, that passion is insufficient. We are not people building scripts, algorithms, and tools; we are people helping people make decisions using technology. We need to relentlessly prioritize outcome.

*"We can't move on until we have an answer to this. If you don't know how this helps him, then how can you sell it? What are his other concerns? What keeps him up at night?"*

*"I have no idea, that's not my job."*

*"Your job is to get this across the finish line, and you can't do that without selling it, so knowing him is absolutely your job."*

We do not work in a vacuum. Executives, product managers, and business leads are the ultimate gatekeepers for our work. The tools and algorithms we develop are shaped by their business understanding to create an impact, or to fulfill the needs of the final customers. These decision-makers ultimately determine whether to implement our work. Why then do we avoid them at all costs? Why, unless they forcefully insert themselves, do we wait until the end of a project to involve them?

According to a study conducted by Deloitte Consulting,[1] over half of the surveyed executives expressed the belief that data science and analytics would fundamentally transform the operations of their businesses. There is overwhelming support and enthusiasm for the practice. Regrettably, most of these initiatives end in failure. In 2018, Gartner found that 85% of such endeavors were unsuccessful.[2] TechRepublic discovered that eight out of ten AI projects had stalled.[3] Similarly, Capgemini revealed that only 27% of big data initiatives were deemed successful.[4] The root cause of these failures does not lie in technical shortcomings, but rather in a lack of communication, strategic alignment, and ultimately, a lack of empathy.

Understanding our stakeholders is crucial for the success of any project. Building a genuine understanding of people, however, is a time-consuming process that cannot be hurried into the final phase of a project. Regrettably, we often regard this step as an afterthought, reacting to feedback and then commending ourselves for operating in an iterative manner. We repeatedly revise and refine our solution after each unsuccessful attempt to gain buy-in from our stakeholders. We misinterpret their needs, work in isolation, make iterative adjustments, and

---

[1] Ammanath, Beena, Susanne Hupfer, and David Jarvis. "Thriving in the Era of Pervasive AI: Deloitte's State of AI in the Enterprise, 3rd Edition." Deloitte Insights, 2020.
[2] White, Andrew. "Our Top Data and Analytics Predictions for 2019." Gartner, 2018.
[3] DeNisco Rayome, Alison. "Why 85% of AI Projects Fail." TechRepublic, 2019.
[4] Capgemini Consulting. "Cracking the Data Conundrum: How Successful Companies Make Big Data Operational." 2015.

become disheartened when projects are eventually abandoned. Ultimately, we have no one to blame but ourselves.

As technology workers, we must allocate as much time to understanding our customers as we do to enhancing our technical expertise.

*"Look, I've known the guy for years, so I'll give you a head start. His position is shaky. He needs to appear to be forward thinking, but he can't have any visible failures. He's popular with the operations side where he came from, but commercial and the CTO consider him a dinosaur. He's out of his depth technically and needs us for a win."*

*"This would give him a win. Other groups have been doing it for years, so all the risks have been uncovered already. It would head off events so we could move more quickly. It would smooth out costs on the operations side as well."*

*"Great, did you tell him any of this the first time?"*

Every person is unique, shaped by their distinct life experiences, varied preferences and aspirations, and diverse value systems. Every facet of their being, from their childhood aspirations to their culinary inclinations, influences and shapes the approximately 35,000 decisions they make each day.[5]

People are an integrated whole; no aspect of their character operates in isolation from the rest. Sharing a name with a childhood bully may subconsciously disadvantage someone in their eyes. Presenting oneself unkempt may evoke memories of an overbearing parent. Drinking black coffee may evoke unconscious responses based on cultural traditions. Avoiding eye

---

[5] Krockow, Eva. "How Many Decisions Do We Make Each Day?" Psychology Today, 2018.

contact may signify distrust in one individual yet convey respect in another. Nervousness, verbal tics, and a feeble handshake may lead them to believe you doubt your own abilities. Stickers on your laptop that signal tribal affiliations to fellow geeks may convey a lack of seriousness to someone unfamiliar with the symbolism. All of these factors can influence your ability to secure their support for a project, irrespective of its potential.

If we accept that our goal is to see our work implemented, then we must learn how to influence our stakeholders. We need to understand their motivations and driving forces. Without a personal understanding of their perspectives, we can only sell to ourselves; absent any insights into their priorities, there is nothing else that we can do.

Technology workers must demonstrate empathy to inspire change.

*"Thanks so much for agreeing to meet me again on this idea."*

*"It's my pleasure. It was really interesting the first time we met, and I'd love to learn more."*

*"If you don't mind my saying so, after a bit of reflection I was a bit concerned I misrepresented what this could do for you and your group, so I wanted to take another crack at it."*

*"It was pretty clear - it sounded like a really neat concept in theory, I'm just not sure we have the bandwidth to be tackling something like that right now, but great initiative and I think it would be great to scope it out a bit for the future."*

*"It's not really a future thing though, most of our peers are either using this or are going to launch in the next couple years. I'm afraid our group could be left behind if we don't move quickly."*

7

*"Really? Why haven't they been talking about it?"*

*"They are being conservative. It has only been soft launches until they get enough data. It's been discussed on the technical side, but once they have a few cycles they will be issuing press releases. If we launch with what I've got though, we can be the first to the party in our area. Let me show you this, it's the results they are seeing in other countries where they have been using the technology for years already after they ironed out all the bugs."*

When a data engineer makes an adjustment that reduces the runtime of a query by a few seconds, they experience great internal satisfaction. Data scientists exchanging algorithms in a model enthusiastically share confusion matrices illustrating the improvement in its predictive power. However, these achievements hold significance solely for us; to the business they are all but invisible. While we should certainly have pride in our work, and pursue excellence, we need to remind ourselves where the value lies.

When technology workers enter university or college, their work is evaluated entirely on a technical basis. The number of lines of code and the elegance of their solutions are ranked by a professor who has provided a discrete, discernible, convergent problem for them to solve, along with a pristine data set.

After their study, they enter the workforce as junior practitioners where they are assigned equally distinct and well-defined tickets at the beginning of every sprint. At each step in their education and career, they are formed into order takers who convert inputs to outputs using understood approaches.

Once these practitioners move on in their careers, their role is no longer to take orders but to work alongside others to analyze a problem and build out a solution. Every measure of their performance from the preceding decade of their working life is discarded. They struggle in this new role and look for ways to delegate their new newfound responsibilities. They remain order takers at a higher level, accepting the requests of stakeholders at face value. They see themselves as intermediaries, simply deconstructing the work, crafting user stories, and assigning tickets to their more junior colleagues. Disinterested in leadership, incapable of influencing team productivity, and detached from the work they love, they become disengaged and pursue new roles.

Technology functions need to break out of this negative feedback loop. Human factors and business advisory skills need to be embedded from the first day of college. Every step of a practitioner's career needs to be oriented towards the creation of value, and this requires a continued and intentional focus on empathy.

Understanding the priorities of decision-makers allows practitioners to not only design an appropriate solution but also to secure their support by framing the benefits in a manner that aligns incentives. Timepieces have beauty through their meticulous engineering, visual design, and usability, but what elevates them from a mere gadget to a luxury item is the emphasis on emotional marketing. Similarly, our work must not just be performant; it must inspire our stakeholders and resonate with them emotionally. We need to put aside the technology, and craft a story where they are the heroes.

*"He wants to get this set up right away. We need to run it in parallel to the current system and figure out for the last two years what the impact would have been if we were using it. He is also afraid our competitors will launch theirs first and wants to be able to share our progress next month at his luncheon."*

*"That's great news - I'll start right away."*

*"You need to delegate the coding though. Right now, you need to write*

*him a brief on where all our competitors are at with this and prepare a few slides and speaking notes for his presentation."*

*"I don't know how much I can delegate; it's been just me for the last year."*

*"I'm going to move somebody over to your team for that. You're also going to have to report weekly to his resource manager, and he's asked his favorite BA to get involved, so make sure that you run everything past her. The PMO will reach out, we're rolling this up to one of next year's strategic initiatives, so you'll need to loop them in. Also, the OCM guy will be reaching out to understand how we'll operationalize this..."*

The reward for a technology worker who has shown him or herself capable of interfacing with business stakeholders is a removal of technical duties. Like a pie eating contest, where the reward is more pie, those who drive change will be given responsibilities they often do not want.

For a geek who has focused on cultivating technical expertise throughout their career, being evaluated on their capacity to build and lead a high functioning team can come as a shock. Unless the individual is naturally inclined towards service, the loss of identity that accompanies a transition to management can make them question their abilities. We forfeit the immediate gratification of coding and debugging for the delayed satisfaction of overseeing multi-year projects.

Dedicated and passionate practitioners, having found personal validation in their work, are now client or stakeholder-facing, and need to leverage a completely new and often undeveloped skillset. This is why so many new managers self-demote within the first year despite initial success. This is also why digital native companies have such non-hierarchical organizational structures, and do not force individual contributors into managerial roles for advancement. The traditional path to promotion becomes irrelevant when the work itself is central to the individual.

New delivery models and development frameworks will not solve the underlying problem. Technology teams are becoming ever-more integrated into the business, and the problem will continue to grow without the conscious introduction of empathy into the technology lexicon. Practitioners need to see their roles as helping others, not blindly implementing technology.

The project I discuss had a successful conclusion. The model was operationalized, and it has exceeded expectations. It is celebrated for the impact it has had on our customers, the reduction in operational cost fluctuations, and is used as evidence of how forward thinking the group is. The underlying model that I spent a year refining remains unacknowledged. The painstaking efforts invested in drift monitoring, error handling, and automated exception reporting, which consumed countless nights and weekends, representing my proudest contributions, was not mentioned in any press releases.

The reality is that nobody cares about the algorithm, the elegant code, or the clever architecture. Unless we can persuade everybody else to favour our technical prowess, upending their business models to implement technical solutions on the basis of their elegance, it will fall to us to adapt to their world. The model I developed had bore no real-world significance as a standalone entity; it was only through its acceptance and deployment that it generated value. Technology workers make their mark in helping others, and to help others we must begin with empathy. Understanding deeply and personally what the motivations, constraints, ambitions, and emotional posture are of the other person. Without this understanding, value creation will be accidental at best.

In the first section of this book, I discuss how the intentional cultivation of empathy can lead to a more successful and satisfying career. Critical for both individual contributors and leaders, this section focuses inward. In the second section, I shift the perspective outward, adopting an enterprise outlook, and illustrate how embedding empathy into a technology function leads to a higher-performing team and organization.

It is my hope that readers will come to see empathy as both a personal characteristic that leads to greater success and mental health, as well as a business asset to be promoted within the technology function. Human factors will be a key differentiator for future practitioners, and geeks with empathy are going to be the change-makers in their organizations.

## Why is this important?

In response to the pandemic, and with a bias for action, corporations are radically flattening their organizational structure, drawing technology workers closer to their stakeholders. To counterbalance their perceived loss of visibility and control, they are also heavily metricizing and monitoring.[6] Leaving their traditional home in a regimented IT stack, software developers, programmers, and analytics professionals are integrating into the organizations they serve.

Simultaneously, centralized IT functions are becoming leaner and transitioning to positions of federated oversight rather than execution. The World Economic Forum asserts that most of the responsibilities entrusted to technology workers today will be assumed by integrated domain experts with broad

---

[6] De Smet, Aaron, Susan Lund, and William Schaninger. "Organizing for the Future." McKinsey Quarterly, 2016.

technical proficiencies.[7] While technical specialists will continue to hold a place in digital native companies and in supporting legacy tools, technical generalists will become more prevalent in traditional organizations.

This transformation has already begun in the field of analytics, where practitioners have been moving for years towards collaborating more closely with their counterparts in the business. Unfortunately, this shift from being an invisible backroom function has exposed a shortcoming in their ability to collaborate. This foreshadows a larger problem for technology workers: increasingly hybrid working arrangements have resulted in reduced face time between teams, which, in conjunction with an escalating reliance on technology and automation, amplifies the need for collaboration. This confluence of factors has captured the attention of McKinsey, which recently reported that foundational skills in the future will not be one's ability to code, but instead one's ability to connect socially.[8]

Technology workers, both new graduates and experienced practitioners, are feeling the results of their of inability to collaborate and are struggling to find their place in organizations that do not understand them. Feeling disenfranchised, ambitious geeks seek more accreditations and greater technical depth. The scripts, programs, and tools that they create are essential, but they are just the way that the practice helps people make decisions. If a technology worker genuinely wants to support their stakeholders, they do not need more certificates; there needs to be mutual trust, mutual understanding, and

---

[7] World Economic Forum. "The Future of Jobs." 2016.
[8] Dondi, Marco, Julia Klier, Frédéric Panier, and Jörg Schubert. "Defining the skills citizens will need in the future world of work." McKinsey, 2021.

above all, empathy.

This work aims to address this gap for both organizations and individuals by examining how to develop, leverage, and demonstrate empathy. By exposing empathy as a key trait and value driver for both practitioners and their organizations, this will help organizations unlock greater value from their technology functions and help individual practitioners differentiate themselves and discover opportunities for advancement.

In simple terms: more value for our stakeholders and more opportunities for us.

### How did we get here?

Several factors contribute to the challenge that technology workers face in establishing strong connections with the business. To understand the current state, we need to go back to the genesis of IT as a distinct organizational function.

When the typing pools of the 1970s gave way to bulky desktop PCs equipped with word processors and digital ledgers, technical support workers were recruited. Their duties included managing printer cables, configuring networks, assisting with forgotten passwords, and setting up computers for new hires. IT did not arrive intentionally, but in response to the business's need to elevate productivity by providing staff with personal computers.

As organizations grew in scale, their dependence on computers increased. More staff digitized, and more technology workers were hired. With this expansion, it was no longer feasible to simply call the computer guy for support. This white glove service was replaced with an email and the requester was added to an informal backlog of work. When the IT team expanded further, even emailing the team to ask for help became a bottleneck, and ticketing systems replaced the personal touch of a phone call or email. At each step of the evolution of the practice, the technology worker became more distant from the person in the business.

Doman-specific tools led to specialization, which pushed us further apart. Proprietary HR and finance platforms were purchased, and the business hired specialists to support these tools. When companies went online, they needed a security function, and hired more specialists. As the technical maturity of corporate life increased, the breadth of IT expanded to meet it. Throughout these developments, the core mentality of order-taking persisted. Whether somebody in the business needs to reset a forgotten password, purchase new software, or land a new data set, it often begins with the impersonal submission of a ticket to an anonymous organizer, who forwarded those tickets to security, ERP, or development as required.

IT was pushed onto organizations as a necessary response to unmet desires. When organizations needed a web presence to maintain relevance, they hired web developers. When organizations began to venture into ecommerce, they invested in a digital practice. In each case, the technology function has been a secondary and often regrettable requirement to enable some business outcome. The balance of power has always favored the business, with the service function expected to execute without question.

It has always been a function without upside; if nothing goes wrong senior leaders will wonder what they are paying for, and if things do go wrong, they will have the same question. Historically, we were not colleagues. In Gene Kim's influential work, *The Unicorn Project*, he captures this sentiment perfectly, writing, "corporate IT is usually viewed as ranks of nameless faces whom you call when there's something wrong with your laptop or when you can't print something."[9]

During the painful digital transformations of legacy organizations, many started to see IT as a strategic differentiator rather than a mere cost center. Influential leaders emerged who could straddle the business and technology realms. These leaders were able to establish credibility on both sides and acted as intermediaries and translators.[10] While organizations began to recognize the function's potential, this realization was primarily the result of the persistent efforts of a select group of individuals, and not through a secular change within the function itself. The practice itself remained isolated order takers, but for the best in class, they were at least taking orders from a knowledgeable intermediary.

Operations research, decision support, and business intelligence were the first technology functions that worked closely with the business. Rather than sending explicit instructions to people that stakeholders would never meet, these ancestral geeks were attending meetings, participating in scoping discussions, and were approached proactively for their opinions. Rebranded to data science and touted as the "sexiest job of the 21st century",[11] these functions experienced a surge in popu-

[9] Kim, Gene. The Unicorn Project: A Novel about Developers, Digital Disruption, and Thriving in the Age of Data. IT Revolution Press, 2019.
[10] Henke, Nicolaus, Jordan Levine, and Paul McInerney. "Analytics Translator: The New Must-Have Role." Harvard Business Review, 2018.
[11] Davenport, Thomas, and DJ Patil. "Data Scientist: The Sexiest Job of the 21st Century." Harvard Business Review, 2018.

larity and raised the expectations of senior executives. However, this new relationship has been overshadowed by a legacy of power imbalance rooted in distinctly different social classes.

Being labeled a "geek" was not always considered a term of endearment. Many of today's senior technology leaders grew up in an era when it was normal to be teased for your technical inclinations. Having a deep knowledge of the Star Wars universe would not earn you a free drink during trivia night; instead, it often led to outright bullying until as recently as the early 2000s. Cosplay would more than hinder your dating possibilities. Positive representation for geeks has only come about recently, and even today, popular television shows such as *The Big Bang Theory*, *The IT Crowd*, or *Silicon Valley* often depict negative stereotypes.

While we can often find some truth in these misrepresentations and laugh at ourselves, they underscore how we are perceived. For most of the history of the tech subculture, we have been maligned outsiders. This station has led to defensiveness and has engrained itself into most business technology functions. We see ourselves as besieged, under-staffed, and under-appreciated.

Several cultural factors have contributed to the current perception of technology workers as eccentric and aloof. These ideas are reinforced by many damaging corporate norms.

### Hiring Practices

The way an organization perceives its technology practice is clear from the job description, the disjointed interview process, and the conveyor belt onboarding.

Immature organizations view technology workers as interchangeable, productive assets, posting checklists of mandatory technology-specific experience levels. They assume that any developer with 5-7 years of JavaScript experience will be essentially the same. The interview process typically involves a written test, a pre-recorded video interview focusing on technical questions, an in-person coding assessment, followed by a perfunctory conversation with the bedraggled hiring manager. If the candidate checks all the right boxes, they are transformed into a corporate resource, added to Jira, and commence their employment.

This dehumanizing and reductive hiring process clearly defines the relationship. Before the geek has even met a single person, they have performed tests and recorded videos. They are a cog in an unknowable machine. Deliver the story points, close your tickets, don't cause a ruckus, and you can stay as long as there is work.

Contrast this with the practices of more progressive and tech-positive organizations, and the differences are stark. Job descriptions from digital native companies emphasize communication and business advisory skills. They outline the required technology stack and, instead of demanding years of experience, look for evidence of capability. Conversations do not end with discussions about company culture; they begin there. Hiring managers involve business leads in meeting new recruits, understand the applicant's aspirations and motivations, and foster a collaborative partnership from the beginning, rather than a transactional association.

Integrating this quality within the organization cannot be an afterthought. Empathy must permeate the technology practice, established as a fundamental value from the first interaction with new hires. Organizations need service-oriented people who are eager to make a change; not the least expensive misanthrope that can close tickets.

## Performance Metrics

There is an often-quoted adage that "what gets measured gets done." This maxim has permeated nearly all management thinking since the beginnings of scientific management in the early 20th century. It represents an apophatic concept - an idea we intuitively grasp but struggle to articulate. We may not be able to change something, but if we can measure it, we feel a sense of control.

Management consultant guru Peter Drucker's version of the quote offers a less concise but more nuanced perspective: "what gets measured gets managed - even when it's pointless to measure and manage it, and even if it harms the purpose of the organization to do so." This gains further dimension through Goodheart's Law, which states, "when a measure becomes a target, it ceases to be a good measure." A related principle, known as Campbell's Law, asserts that "the more a metric counts for real decisions, the greater the pressure for corruption, the more it distorts the situation it's intended to monitor."

We measure performance for all the right reasons. We want a sense of control, even if that control is illusory. We also want to encourage our teams and we find that the desire to win is heightened when healthy rivalry and time pressure coincide.[12]

Measuring something sparks that sense of rivalry and can lead to more motivated workers, but it needs to be something within their control. Making them accountable for something that they cannot manage can have the opposite effect. The

---

[12] Malhotra, Deepak. "The Desire to Win: The Effects of Competitive Arousal on Motivation and Behavior." Organizational Behavior and Human Decision Processes 111, no. 2 (March 2010): 139–146.

worst case is when they are measured against an incorrectly assumed proxy for value.

When senior leaders with a loose grasp on how technology functions add value to their organizations are charged with devising operational frameworks, they gravitate toward tangible outputs. Executive leaders inaugurate the formation of an analytics function by setting targets for the number of proof-of-concept projects. Business intelligence leaders, responding to the prior year's opportunities, reactively create performance indicators tied to response time. Executives overseeing groups of software developers, aching to prove productivity increases, measure the story points executed in a sprint, tickets closed, or, alarmingly, lines of code.

These business metrics certainly encourage output, as defined. They also give executives a very digestible metric in terms of the percent annual increase, and an opportunity to showcase their ability to improve performance in their stack. However, there is nothing in these metrics that direct that output towards a meaningful end.

When we tell practitioners that their measure of performance is the number of experimental proof of concepts, practitioners are incented to blindly fire off deliverables rather than take the time to evaluate whether it should even be performed. When bonuses are being decided, having a ninetieth percentile average scrum velocity will land you a ninetieth percentile bonus; questioning the product owner will land you an uncomfortable conversation about teamwork and role expectations. We make our code less elegant to have more lines on our scorecard, and we oversize our user stories so that we have a higher sprint velocity. Focusing on gaming the metrics of the practice ultimately destroys value, despite productivity rising on the executive's scorecard.

In his depiction of Victorian factories, Marx wrote about work that "mutilated the laborer into a fragment of a man, degrad[ing] him to the level of an appendage of a machine, destroy[ing] every remnant of charm in his work and turn[ing] it into hated toil."[13] This characterization could easily apply to modern technology workers. Rather than working together with their peers to achieve a goal none could accomplish independently, they channel their efforts into a ticket management system, a depersonalizing intermediary between frustrated and isolated people. Any indication of critical thinking is punished, until every geek settles into their station as a pliant appendage.

Performance metrics are intended to encourage positive behaviors in staff, and to provide management a way of evaluating the value that is created. When technology metrics are explicitly and exclusively based on output, the message is clear: you are a productive asset, and your worth is your output. We need to step back and ask whether that output is valuable. We need to assess our work based on its contribution to the organizational goals.

## Compensation

Misunderstood individual contributors, hired based on their years of experience with each technology, directed towards blind production, are compensated in an equally transactional way. Lockstep pay-bands based on experience are adjusted with annual cost-of-living increments. Occasionally, organizations will provide small, long-vested options to avoid the costs and disruptions that would attend a high churn team. For those

---

[13] Marx, Karl. Das Kapital: A Critique of Political Economy. Benediction Classics, 2019. Originally published as volumes in 1867, 1885, and 1894.

with remote work arrangements, they may find their salary adjusted based on their location; their salary is not negotiated in good faith based on the applicant's potential, it is determined by the corporation who chooses the quality of life that their staff is entitled to. Occasional market surveys ensure that paybands are aligned to comparable organizations. If the geeks continue to produce, they receive their wages.

If an organization decides to invest in the practice and create senior leadership roles specific to technology workers, those who have moved up through the organization face a new compensation program often based on value drivers and a combination of incentives. Now, rather than being evaluated on output, they are evaluated on the delivery of key projects.

Having dedicated their career to execution rather than design, they find themselves lost as to how to be successful. Typically, they default to their training, and their management style mirrors their prior experiences, focusing on process over product. While they conscientiously complete all HR-mandated leadership training, the only tangible support that they can offer their team is a peer review. Their servant leadership accreditation goes in the same drawer as their other forgotten certifications.

In the end, leadership ability becomes muddled with project management, and the new manager sees his or her role as putting out work. That changes the practice into an assembly line, eliminating creativity. When we compensate based on a faulty proxy for value, we incentivize the wrong things.

### Education

Writing a bubble sort function in Java, memorizing archaic

frameworks, and mastering advanced calculus are rites of passage for computer science graduates. Data science graduate students normalize data, perform principal component analysis, and interpolate missing values. Those with an organizational focus slot simple stories into epics and oversee virtual projects in a kabuki reenactment of a predictable project. The education of geeks is primarily designed for ease of grading, rather than to prepare them for real life.

Every seasoned technology worker has seen the look of confused terror on a new analyst's face when they encounter their first dirty data set. Every developer has experienced situations where they have delivered what a stakeholder requested, but not what they truly wanted. When the tractable and predictable world of academia is replaced with the messiness of real life, they need to quickly retool; otherwise, they will flounder.

Employers are equally frustrated. They often express concerns about the lack of soft skills in university graduates.[14] Academia's response has been to adjust the curriculum, incorporating communication and leadership courses. Rather than emphasizing experiential learning, they formalize even human interaction, replacing empathy with more procedural decision frameworks.

Universities have a mandate to produce broadly educated and intellectually curious adults. Curricula are designed to encourage students to enroll in courses from various subjects, with the hope that they will acquire foundational knowledge and the ability to think critically about issues. While this approach contributes to building a well-rounded citizenry, it does

---

[14] Stirrett, Scott. "When Hiring New Grads, Employers Should Ignore Grade Point Average." Globe and Mail, July 2, 2019.

not always equip students for immediate and productive employment.[15] Traditional liberally educated students make great neighbors, but rarely are they equipped for their future work in technology. The coursework for formally educated geeks is based on well-intentioned societal aspirations rather than preparation for the working world.

In *Goodbye to All That*, Robert Graves writes, "It is only recently that I have overcome my education and gone back too that early institutional spontaneity."[16] We need to rethink how we prepare these students, and for those who have already been influenced by this deterministic approach, to find creative ways to undo the damage that has been caused.

## Technical Maturity

We have all been conditioned to believe that technical maturity, often a euphemism for complexity, is a valuable metric in its own right. It is commonly believed that, all else being equal, it is better to be more technically advanced than less. With a goal so vague as this, several consultancies and popular business authors have come up with their own expensive assessments that depend, necessarily, on self-attested and subjective questions about how the entity leverages technology.

Sitting through a formal survey, we answer superficial questions to establish our ranking on their benchmark. Do you have the data you need to make effective decisions? Did your

[15] Bok, Derek. Our Underachieving Colleges: A Candid Look at How Much Students Learn and Why They Should Be Learning More. Princeton University Press, 2008.
[16] Graves, Robert. Goodbye to All That. Everyman's Library, 2018.

organization invest more in IT than it did last year? Do you have strategic technology initiatives planned for the next year? Are you using modern tooling and infrastructure? When we go down this path, we carelessly define the technical maturity of an entity as the number of tools and the size of the IT team and open the door to more expensive assessments by consultants. No connection is made between technical maturity and the ability of an organization to execute. The relationship is murky and confuses correlation with causation.

A parallel can be drawn with a celebrated horse from Germany in the late 19th century named Clever Hans, who was believed to be a mathematical genius. During performances, Han's handler would stand beside him, taking math questions from an enthusiastic audience. Hans would appear to consider the questions for a moment, then carefully tap his hoof to arrive at the correct answer. The audience would applaud, and the horse would be rewarded with a treat. People soon realized that if the handler and audience did not react, Hans would continue tapping his hoof until he received his treat.[17] The horse was not a genius; it simply understood that persistent tapping would garner excitement and the desired reward.

This anecdote serves as a reflection of our own cyclical technology transformations. Unable to produce benefit or meet the expectations of our stakeholders, we are given a mandate to improve our technical maturity. Consultants assess us against a proprietary benchmark and present a prioritized list of recommendations. Carefully, we tap our hoofs, waiting for the crowd to cheer. Our maturity score rises a few points on their chart, but there is no organizational impact.

Despite adopting Agile methodologies, expanding our

---

[17] Pfungst Oskar, Clever Hans. Pfungst, 1911.

teams, and migrating to cloud-based systems, our companies still run on Excel. We can convince our strategic projects team and the finance department that we need funding for a new data governance tool, but we have not added a penny to the bottom line. We have become more mature while our organizations have not advanced in decades. With completely misaligned priorities, we have met the goals they have given us at their own expense.

## Change Management

Organizational change management professionals are skilled at guiding people through the transition process. They build urgency around the change, establishing need, and they craft a story where the participant has the potential to be the hero. Done well, they can encourage people to walk happily to where they are directed. Even though seasoned employees can see the cue cards, the theatrics and the energy make it a positive experience.

Contrasting that polished function to the way that most technical initiatives are implemented, where the purpose of change management is reducing discomfort, is dismal. We put the technology on a pedestal and usher people quickly past it, hoping they do not touch anything on the way.

Rather than excitement at the chance to partner on an interesting and important project, both the geeks and the business leaders brace themselves with apprehension. IT knows the people in the business will have unrealistic expectations, while the business knows IT will give them a solution they cannot use. Reflecting on past experience, leaders do all they can to mitigate risks, imposing an intricate list of requirements and conditions. Without mutual trust and understanding, change management has become pain management.

## Geeks with Empathy

Why is it important that geeks develop empathy? Is it to direct our efforts to more effective ends? It's true, but that does not appeal to most of us, and there is no romance in that. Is it that our mental and physical health will increase? That's true as well, even if a bit patronizing. Is it that we will create more value for our organizations? That's true too, but as most of us already feel we are not receiving our due respect, that likely is not the most important piece either. Though all of these are true the ultimate reason is that we geeks had no say in the current paradigm, and I would like to see us take control of our profession.

We have inherited standardized corporate procedures established by uninformed executives in the 1970s and have resigned ourselves to accepting them as the only viable approach. We have an opportunity to stand up, design our own working conditions, and say we are not backroom technical resources, we are going to influence the way that our organizations are run.

This book is not intended to be a bitter jeremiad against technical specialists, doomed to failure by their inadequacy. It does not aim to paint a bleak picture of business stakeholders as desirous creatures bound by ignorance and fear. The intention is to shine a light on a better path for those who pursue empathy. Replacing the caricature of dozens of unblinking grumps in ergonomic chairs with that of affable techies who solve problems. It aims to help us genuinely connect with our peers and find true joy in those partnerships.

INTRODUCTION

However, this change will not come about on its own. Legacy organizations will continue to tighten their controls, fragmenting technical work into increasingly minute tasks, while anonymous resources shift between companies, adjusting to new time zones and email domains. Improvement requires the concerted effort of geeks willing to step beyond their comfort zones and earnestly strive to comprehend the perspectives of their stakeholders.

We are, by and large, technological determinists. Sometimes this takes a quasi-religious form in a satisfied anticipation of the singularity, sometimes an ascetic self-denial through a life of the mind. Stationed behind a bank of monitors, some of us see ourselves as, in the words of Marvin Minsky, "meat machines,"[18] identifying more with our tools than our colleagues. This viewpoint, depicting humans as an organic version of a pure digital information processing unit, is flawed and leads to a perverse grand fantasy.[19] Many of us, harboring those inclinations, prefer to withdraw from society, finding solace in reasoning that aligns with our social standing and reduces cognitive dissonance.

The alternative, though uncomfortable, is infinitely rewarding. We need to change our self-perception from that of intelligent outsiders guiding unenlightened stakeholders to that of partners; people helping other people to accomplish their goals. When we see ourselves not just as implementors of new

[18] Weizenbaum, Joseph. On the Impact of the Computer on Society. Science. 176,609-614, 1972. The 'meat machine' quote was attributed to Minsky 36 years later in an article for the journal, IEEE Annals of the History of Computing.
[19] Weizenbaum, Joseph. Computer Power and Human Reason. W. H. Freeman and Company, 1976.

technologies but as enablers and supporters, we reprogram ourselves to seek out opportunities to help. Humans are created for community and for service, and when we set that as our north star, we become not just personally happier and healthier, but we are more successful in our careers.

This needs to begin with empathy. The successful technology workers of tomorrow will not be the 10x developers, they will be those who can build meaningful relationships with their clients and colleagues, and to see the world through their eyes.

Becoming empathetic is not a matter of instituting a new change management framework. We cannot accomplish it by adding "human factors" as a consideration during requirements gathering. It requires personal reflection and an intentional redirection of our focus. The goal of this work is to build a foundation for that reflection in the reader, and to establish empathy as a critical factor for personal and professional success.

# BEING EMPATHETIC

*"Thank you for that demo. We really appreciate the work you and the team put into it. I do have a question, or more of a comment, and I'm trying to find the words, so this doesn't come across as disrespectful or dismissive.*

*I've been at this a while. Around the table here, probably 200 years of experience. We all do our development hours, we attend conferences, we keep relevant. We know what our competitors do, and it's the same as what we do.*

*So, what I'm saying, respectfully, is what makes you think in the last six months you guys discovered a better way to do this than the thousands of people who actually do this for a living?"*

Geeks will always be confronted with detractors and their weak appeals to tradition with the chorus, "we've always done it this way." When our recommendations are challenged, we are left with a choice: do we respectfully reaffirm our position, weather the discomfort of a potentially tense social situation, or yield to the weight of their experience? Often, in the face of this social pressure, we find ourselves conceding, convinced that we should seek executive sponsorship. We hope that others will fight our battles for us so that we can concentrate on the less adversarial aspects of the project, where our skills and interests lie.

In the experience I described in the introduction, my leader pushed me to realize that the business sponsor did not need mathematical rigor – what he needed was an understanding of how our proposal aligned with his personal objectives. This invaluable insight led to a new default approach: for each project, I would focus on the business goals, gloss over the technical details, and assume that success would naturally follow.

Being a process-driven person by nature, I simply replaced one framework for another.

*"Thanks for the question – that's definitely a great point and one that I'll back out a bit and look at in terms of process. There's no change here, it's the exact approach you have always used. It's completely in line with professional standards and is still what your peers do.*

*The only change is that we automate some parts and reduce the workload for analysts so they can focus on more value-added activities. Your teams will be more productive in the end."*

In a popular math joke, a teacher enters the school gymnasium and sees the principal staring up at the ceiling. The teacher hears the principal quietly counting so asks what he is doing. The principal responds, "I need to know how many lights are in here to validate a contractors estimate." The math teacher quickly multiplies the ten rows by the eight columns and says, "there are eighty lights." The principal sighs and tells him, "thank you, but I need an exact number."

When we are in a situation requiring salesmanship, we often deploy calcified processes rather than allowing situational fluidity. We diligently study change management frameworks and return to our tasks with a newfound sense of assurance in our approach. We do not consider the stakeholder as a person with a perspective, but as a box in a flowchart. We become like pre-sales engineers following a script. Unless we recognize ours as a service profession, and empathy one of our tools, we can quickly fall into the same patterns of thinking that we find frustrating about our stakeholders.

Every individual has unique motivations and if we do not understand the person, we will not be able to identify the specific factors that drive their decisions. Some may be motivated by technical prowess, while others prioritize risk management or business outcome. To effectively navigate such diverse motivations, we must remain adaptable in our approach and tailor our strategies to suit the situation.

*"That makes sense and I appreciate the clarity; it has really helped me to better see where the disconnect is. You just don't understand our business overall and how this group fits in.*

*Our team is like a nursery for people pursuing their financial analyst certification. In their rotation, they will all spend at least a year here to get familiar with our processes. We can't automate that, or they will not be able to understand it in the end. Our future leaders will have less understanding than they do today.*

*Second point is that this is absolutely mission critical. We cannot rely on programs to do this for us. The consequences if we get it wrong are too great.*

*I wonder too, where is the end of all this automation? Who is going to run the company? It's short sighted. We might be more profitable for a couple years, but it will be a disaster in the long term."*

The messaging beneath the superficially polite post-presentation conversation is quite clear. The senior leader is not going to bite, and the technical team's influence has been diminished. The concerns underlying the rejection are so scattered that they cannot be adequately addressed in a group discussion. The stakeholder's objections range from hubris to risk to larger social implications and employee retention.

The project, conducted on behalf of a prominent financial institution, was to replace an error-prone and highly manual process with an automated system that would directly source data. The automation would effectively eliminate the risks associated with human error. Since it was such a tedious and time-consuming task, the analysts responsible for the process would be happier, and would have more time available for other work. Almost no consideration was given to change management or communication for this simple project because there was no conceivable downside. It was expected to be an effortless victory.

Following the conversation, the team, visibly disheartened and frustrated, concluded with a routine listing of key takeaways before snapping closed their laptops. During a subsequent debrief, the depth of their disappointment and exasperation became apparent.

*"What was that? Why did so many senior people even show up? It was such a simple project!"*

*"I'm so sick of this, they are more likely to lose people because they are making them spend six months copying and pasting in Excel than they are by automating that."*

*"I still don't understand his objections, he was all over the place and his team didn't say anything, but I know most of them agree with us."*

The meeting became an ambush, and the geeks who were expecting a simple approval to proceed lost face in front of key people in the organization. Morale was impacted, and the team naturally became less trusting of their customers, turned inward, and became more insular.

The orchestrator of the ambush, a highly esteemed and influential figure within the organization, unwittingly became the subject of unfiltered derision among the members of the technology team. Following the meeting, a number of his peers discreetly approached the technology team, urging them to push forward with the proposed changes, assuring them that they would take care of any fallout.

Two months later, the retirement of that leader was announced, and six months later he left the company that he served for the previous forty years. His legacy was sound, his career admired, and at his retirement party several leaders shared stories about how his mentorship changed their lives. There was an article in a professional publication listing his accomplishments in his industry and community. The news of his retirement, and litany of his contributions, was shared with the team. On hearing what a great man he was, their original mirth at his departure turned into shame. We had reduced him to an obstacle in the path of our small project, completely unaware of the impact he had.

During a private conversation, I gained insight into the rationale behind his objections.

*"I was really surprised to hear how many people he helped in his career. I only crossed paths with him a few times, and after he railroaded our team at that meeting, I thought he was just a bitter old man who was scared of progress."*

*"Well look at it from his perspective. He knew he was retiring within*

*a year and you guys showed up and told him you were going to automate processes that he created at the start of his career. You also gave some euphemisms for layoffs. He was trying to protect his team. All you needed to do was get one of the analysts to walk him through it before the meeting, which is what I ended up doing with him."*

When an appeal to mathematical rigor no longer worked, I began to focus on the business outcome. When the business outcome did not work, I assumed it was insurmountable, and considered the person an enemy. This challenging experience taught me a valuable lesson: there is no one-size-fits-all strategy when it comes to engaging with others. If we hope to advance projects successfully, we must tailor our approach to the unique motivations of the gatekeepers involved.

If there is any positive aspect to this regrettable incident, it is that each participant emerged from the project with a profound determination to empathize with their respective stakeholders. While the disparaging remarks and gossip within our small technical function did little to diminish the notable achievements of the esteemed leader, the sense of shame stemming from their newfound understanding did foster a renewed focus and resilience among the analysts.

The empathetic geek is not just a more valuable employee, he or she is a happier and more self-actualized person.

## Cognitive Empathy

In *Don't Look Up*, Dr. Mindy, portrayed by Leonardo Di-Caprio, struggles to convey the gravity of an impending meteor impact to the president. In an attempt to bolster his case and establish credibility, he delves into the technical details, stating, "[the meteor] came from the Oort cloud, which is the outermost part of the solar system. Using Gauss's method of orbital determination [...]" Unable to read the president's body language, she eventually has to ask him directly to adjust his approach.

After multiple requests for clarity, co-presenter Rob Morgan intervenes with, "Madam President, this comet is what we call a planet-killer." The visceral explanation shifts the tone of the conversation, allowing it to proceed more constructively with the severity of the situation established.

This kind of scenario, generally with lower stakes, is not uncommon for technology workers. When we are questioned about an aspect of our project, we bashfully approach the whiteboard and provide a primer on back propagation or distributed computing. We try to be transparent but end up confusing and irritating our clients, then we respond by providing further detail. This back-and-forth can lead to an uncomfortable escalation, reinforcing mutual preconceptions. Unlike Dr. Mindy, we often lack a "Rob Morgan" to rescue us, highlighting the need to exercise cognitive empathy.

## What is Cognitive Empathy

Cognitive empathy is the capacity of an individual to perceive and understand what other people are feeling. It does not require an emotional response (psychopaths are great at cognitive empathy) it only demands that the individual be able to imagine for a moment that they were the other person. For a healthy child, this capability naturally develops around the age of three. Parents reinforce this with reminders like, "would you want Tony to share his toy with you?" While this comes easier to some than others, people, in general, have an in-built understanding of the theory of mind and can ascribe a mental state to another person.

Quite often, left-brained logical thinkers need to be mindful of their tendency to disregard the human factors. For instance, when a friend confides in us that they were turned down for a promotion at work, our inner engineer may leap into problem-solving mode. With the best of intentions, we may highlight all the issues that led to this result and start ideating on how to prepare for a better future outcome.

However, if we take a moment to imagine the mental state of the other person, our approach would change. We would reflect on what a person suffering a professional setback and personal defeat wants to hear, and we would correctly respond by offering a sympathetic ear. We realize that we need to wait; problem-solving can come once the wounds heal.

People are not rational actors; they are guided by very simple maxims. When we shift from our logical environments, where we interact with bash scripts and DevOps, to the random and emotional realm of human interactions, our approaches break down.

Beneath our veneer of civility and intellect is an animalistic and intuitive creature. In Paul MacLean's triune brain model,[20] he describes our minds as a Venn diagram; a neocortex governing logic and higher thinking overlaying a limbic system which controls emotions. At the core of these two systems is a reptilian brain concerned only with our base instincts and survival.

---

[20] MacLean, Paul. The Triune Brain in Evolution: Role in Paleocerebral Functions. Springer Science & Business Media, 1990.

While this model is disputed by some modern psychologists, it goes some way towards describing the interaction between these structures. Like a matryoshka doll of conflicting thought processes, it highlights the struggle that people face in overcoming, or at least subduing, their reptilian and limbic systems. To approach a situation truly rationally we need to pacify the larger part of our psychology and overcome base instincts. When we're dealing with a stakeholder whose reptile brain is engaged, we need to calm those urges before we move on.

In *The Lucifer Principle*, author Howard Bloom builds on this triune brain concept to make a case that this internal struggle not only impacts the individual but is perhaps the single guiding force for human development. Competition between groups of people, guided by their base instincts, has led to a superorganism at the macro level, while at the micro level, competition between individuals creates a pecking order that has become our social fabric.[21] One frightening conclusion of this thesis is that what we consider evil is a natural byproduct of our genetics. The more optimistic take is that the motive force of this internal and external conflict stirs ambition and creativity.

As much as geeks would prefer otherwise, people are instinctual and fickle. An illustrative example is the ultimatum game, a well-known economic experiment.[22] In this zero-sum game, two participants are involved. The first participant receives ten dollars, a portion of which can be allocated to the

[21] Bloom, Howard. The Lucifer Principle: A Scientific Expedition into the Forces of History. Atlantic Monthly Press, 1995.
[22] Harsanyi, John C. 1961. On the Rationality Postulates underlying the Theory of Cooperative Games. The Journal of Conflict Resolution. 5 (2): 179–196.

second participant. If the second participant decides their portion is unfair, they can reject the offer, resulting in no gain for either party. The first participant is motivated to offer the minimum amount to prevent rejection, while the second participant decides whether to accept the money or forgo it to penalize the first participant. Despite the rational choice for the second person being to accept any offer, individuals are often willing to sacrifice monetary gain to penalize what they perceive as an unfair offer.

Variations of this experiment were conducted for decades, highlighting several interesting behavioral traits. In a notable 2003 variation that replicated the original experiment, the second participant underwent an MRI, offering researchers insight into the neural activity accompanying decisions to accept or reject an offer.[23]

When the participant received a lowball offer, the insula cortex was activated. This primitive part of the brain normally deals with pain and smells, signaling that the recipient has literal disgust at the offer. Conversely, a more generous offer triggered activation in the prefrontal cortex, associated with logical thinking. In both cases, brain activity occurred before a conscious decision was reached. Though the participants would certainly feel that they took all factors into account in making their decision, their brain had already decided for them. Emotionality impacts decision making more than logic.

As participants in this intricate social dance, we cannot recuse ourselves without suffering personal consequences. We are all just a thin membrane of sentience stretched over the

---

[23] Sanfey AG, Rilling JK, Aronson JA, Nystrom LE, Cohen JD. The neural basis of economic decision-making in the Ultimatum Game. Science. 2003 Jun 13;300(5626):1755-8.

brain of an angry primate. When we interface with our customers, colleagues, or clients, rather than seeing them as an obstacle to overcome as part of our deliverables, we need to see them as a person to understand and support – for our sake as much as for theirs.

Throughout history, there were periods when individuals could set aside personal needs for the greater good, aligning themselves with various social groups such as church, neighborhood, state, and country. Religiosity and nationalism facilitated the overcoming of natural instincts through social reinforcement. However, ours is a time marked by hyper-individualism and increasing selfishness.

A Gallup poll indicates a significant shift, with the percentage of people considering themselves the primary concern in decision-making rising from 12% in the 1950s to over 80% in the 1980s.[24] We celebrate people for their popularity rather than their accomplishments, and we seek attention for its own sake rather than as an outcome of our efforts. People are selfish, impulsive, and emotional, by nature; we rationalize that with mindsets and belief systems that assign an appropriate and supportive worldview.[25]

In the 1920s, in response to the then-dominant theory of social Darwinism, Frank Boas put forward the theory that human behavior is not rooted in biology but was an entirely social construct. That concept of cultural relativity, dominant and unassailable today, blinds us to biological factors. We cannot ignore our biology, or fight it on philosophical grounds, without

[24] Twenge, Jean, and Keith Campbell. The Narcissism Epidemic: Living in the Age of Entitlement. Atria Books, 2010.
[25] Simler, Kevin, and Robin Hanson. The Elephant in the Brain: Hidden Motives in Everyday Life. Oxford University Press, 2017.

consequences.

The default orientation towards selfishness may be supported by current cultural norms, but it is not something we cannot overcome. With effort, we can conquer these instincts and reorient ourselves to practice empathy and realize all the personal and professional benefits that entails.

Beyond a conscious attempt to see situations from the other persons perspective, the largest part of establishing and cultivating cognitive empathy is building an understanding of the human decision-making process and the factors governing our behavior.

### Decision Making

Neoclassical economists use the term "homo economicus" to depict a theoretical abstraction of a human being. This abstraction is characterized by making rational decisions at every point in life, consistently seeking to maximize marginal utility. This concept, based on the work of John Stuart Mill claims that every individual, at every moment of the day, will assess their competing priorities and make an instantaneous and logic choice; if at the moment they assign more value to an hour of leisure than the wage they would receive for an hour of work, they will instantly put down their tools.[26] Once hunger or boredom changes the calculus, they will be prompted to return to work.

Like a physicist assuming a spherical frictionless cow, this

---

[26] Originally published in his "Essays on some unanswered questions of political economy" in 1844. See also, "On the logic of the moral sciences" originally published in "A System of logic", first published in 1844.

simplification offers only a directional understanding of motivating factors and does not align with reality, as evidenced by our own lived experiences. In contrast, behavioral economics delves into the influence of psychological, emotional, cultural, and social factors on decision making, exploring the circumstances under which irrationality will surface.

A key insight emerging from behavioral economics is the relativity inherent in all decisions. H.L. Mencken said, more than a little anachronistically, "a wealthy man is one who earns $100 a year more than his wife's sister's husband." We do not feel poor unless we see opulence, and we do not realize our blessings until we feel their absence.

Organizations use this to great effect when they are developing their pricing strategy. Consumers, with no way to know how much an item should cost, look at the alternatives available to determine worth. This "coherent arbitrariness" is exploited by companies who include very expensive options not with the expectation of selling them, but to raise the perceived value for the intended product.

In *Priceless: The Myth of Fair Value*, author William Poundstone provides examples of how stores can increase individuals' willingness to pay through clever misdirection.[27] For instance, Broadway venues will price a few prime seats orders of magnitude higher than the mid-tier seats that constitute most of the available product. Consumers, seeing that seats are available for $1000, $100, and $60, choose the $100 seats, believing they have secured $900 in savings. The presence of the $1000 decoy influences this decision. Without it, the majority would opt for the $60 seats, perceiving them as a good deal

---

[27] Poundstone, William. Priceless: The Myth of Fair Value. Hill and Wang, 2011.

over the premium $100 seats, yielding only a $40 saving. Similar strategies manifest in subscription services, where bundled goods enhance the perceived value, even if the bundled items would not be individually purchased. Luxury goods stores prominently display items like a $70,000 watch, not necessarily for sale, but to make a $10,000 timepiece seem like a compelling deal.

In our world, this strategy can be applied by consistently presenting a spectrum of options, guiding decision-makers toward the most preferred choice. When sharing an RFP with potential proponents, including elite-tier consultancies raises the ceiling, making the preferred consultancy a more evident and favorable choice to decision makers.

In the philosophical thought experiment named after the 14th century French philosopher Jean Buridan, a hungry donkey enters a barn and finds itself equidistant between two bales of hay. The donkey, unable to decide, eventually succumbs to starvation.[28] As geeks, it is our responsibility to aid the donkey by moving the inferior bale of hay further from the indecisive creature.

Similarly, our stakeholders, lacking a basis to assess value, encounter challenges in evaluating fairness. In a study by Kahneman and Knetsch, participants were asked to categorize price increases as fair or unfair to understand the criteria under which the public would consider them justified. What they found was that regardless of the reasons, whether increased profitability for the vendor, rising input costs, or unavoidable external price shocks, increased taxes, respondents considered

---

[28] Knowles, Elizabeth. The Oxford Dictionary of Phrase and Fable. Oxford University Press, 2005.

any reason unfair.[29] In other words, we cannot explain away failures solely in terms of cost or schedule misses; stakeholders and project sponsors will perceive the situation as unfair to them. Establishing a robust risk registry along with mitigations is crucial to diminishing the emotional impact resulting from accepted scope or cost creep.

Another interesting insight is that people tend to be happier with three $1,000 bonuses than with a single $3,000 bonus.[30] Often, even if the value of a single item is higher than the aggregate value of several smaller items, the reported satisfaction of the recipient is higher if received separately. The key takeaway is that the empathetic geek should not "wrap all their Christmas presents in one box" but should instead separate the benefits and gradually introduce them throughout the course of an engagement. Rather than delivering a final product at the end of an extended project, seek ways to provide sneak peeks and iterative value along the way, creating the perception of quicker progress and delighting the project sponsor.

People also feel more confident in a decision if they have a sense of control. If stakeholders are presented with a fully developed plan for their approval, they will instinctively want to adjust some part of it to make it their own. Designers have cleverly exploited this through a "hairy arm" technique. This term comes from wedding photographers who, when present-

---

[29] Kahneman, Daniel, Jack L. Knetsch, and Richard Thaler. "Fairness as a Constraint on Profit Seeking: Entitlements in the Market." The American Economic Review, Sep., 1986, Vol. 76, No. 4, pp. 728-741.
[30] Shirai, Miyuri. Effects of Quality and Price Appeals on Consumers' Internal Reference Prices and Quality Perceptions. Modern Economy. 05. 831-840, 2014.

ing the proposed collection to discerning clients, include a photograph that is a close-up of a hairy arm. The clients immediately ask for that photo to be removed from the collection. Satisfied that they have left their mark, they then approve the remainder. Including a "hairy arm" in a proposal and guiding stakeholders toward removing it gives them a sense of control and ensures that they don't try to make their mark on a more impactful area.

Used judiciously, these insights into decision-making can help guide stakeholders down a path we have created for them. However, it is crucial to distinguish between those parts of a project that require deep collaboration, such as operationalization, and what is clearly in the geek's domain. The ultimate goal should be reducing friction in decision-making, not overt manipulation. This differentiation and the risk of perceived manipulation become clearer when one appreciates the nature of the relationship between the participants.

Beyond having practical applicability, these studies clearly show that decision making is not the logical process we would expect from "homo economicus". People are guided by forces that they do not themselves understand. Realizing this, we can avoid the pitfalls that come from logical proposals and reframe our narrative. We must also understand that decision-making by stakeholders takes place within different frameworks, depending on the implicit relationship.

### Social vs. Market Contract

With natural myopia, we assume that people who do not have the same value system or beliefs as us are simply in error. If we are being charitable, we give them the benefit of the doubt and assume it is because they are misinformed. We desire predictability and often wish our stakeholders would act more logically. However, that logical behavior, or market contract framework, only pits us against each other. We are in a much better position if we can operate within a social contract. Once an interaction moves to a market interaction, though the counterparty may act more rationally, it will always be to their own benefit.

Under a social contract, people will try to find a mutually beneficial outcome. Behavioral economist Dan Ariely writes of a daycare that introduced an additional fee for those who were late picking up their children.[31] Before that business decision, parents would feel personally motivated to get their children on time to avoid inconveniencing the staff. Now that guilt was not a motivator, late pickups increased because it became a transactional relationship. Parents would assess whether it was worth it to pay the fee to work for an extra hour, and often decide it was.

When the daycare saw that their new policy had backfired, they eliminated late pickups fees with the expectation that things would return to normal. Customers were now in a market contract state of mind, and the social norms had been discarded. The removal of late pickup fees just made it an even better deal, so late pickups increased still further.

It is very difficult to move from a market contract to a social contract, but the reverse can be instantaneous. We need to be always aware of the relationships we are fostering and seek to cultivate mutual respect. Having a pragmatic and logical relationship may sound great in theory, but in practice, it makes

---

[31] Ariely, Dan. Predictably Irrational, Revised and Expanded Edition: The Hidden Forces That Shape Our Decisions. Harper Perennial, 2010.

relationships transactional.

Crafting an engagement under a social contract can begin with something as simple as using deferential and respectful speech. People find a great deal of satisfaction and self-respect in their work, and any statements or actions that diminish the value of their work is taken as a personal attack.

During a study of an elder care home in San Francisco by Arlie Hochschild, a group of widows, bored with their ceaseless leisure, organized a small working group that crafted items to sell. They reported that this activity brought a sense of dignity to their lives. At one point, a group member asked to keep a few of the crafts as gifts for her family. This implication that what they were doing was not work but rather a hobby broke the perception of it being dignified work. The group did not recover from this slight, and the requestor was forced out. We need to show respect for the work of others and be mindful of actions that could be seen as dismissive or devaluing.[32] The work of geeks often replaces or augments existing processes; we need to be mindful that we do not undermine something that provides them dignity.

We are frequent recipients of these slights and are less forgiving than we expect our stakeholders to be. We are stuck in our ways because we justify our positions and reinforce our outsider mentality through these slights. That self-justification is necessary; it lets us live with our decisions and failures. Without it we would not be able to sleep – we would be constantly second guessing ourselves. However, this self-justification prevents objectivity and hinders our ability to change views, approaches, or take responsibility for our actions. Like our

---

[32] Hochschild, Arlie Russel. The Unexpected Community. Prentice-Hall, 1973.

stakeholders, we have biases, but we hesitate to be the one to adjust. We believe our beliefs and perceptions are accurate and unbiased, a phenomenon known as naïve realism.[33]

This tendency is natural because arriving at a position involves full reflection and self-interrogation. Since we can't fully know the minds of others, we only see their opinions and output.[34]

Moreover, we're biased in that we only see the current state and not the events leading up to it. The benevolent dolphin problem illustrates this. We often hear of shipwrecked sailors nudged towards safety by saintly dolphins, leading us to believe they are naturally good. However, we don't know how many sailors they pushed to their deaths further out to sea. Similarly, we don't know how many times our stakeholders were let down by our predecessors or how many times, in past roles, they had to fight with IT. We just assume that they are evil dolphins.

When we distance ourselves from stakeholders in an attempt to establish a professional working relationship, we replace a social contract with a market contract. We cannot let the allure of a purely logical exchange shift us away from a relationship where we can be both more effective and personally satisfied.

We need to be aware however, that besides the logical fallacies that guide our decision making, and the implicit social

---

[33] Ehrlinger J., T. Gilovich, and L. Ross. Peering into the bias blind spot: people's assessments of bias in themselves and others. Pers Soc Psychol Bull. 2005 May;31(5):680-92.

[34] Pronin E, T. Gilovich, and L. Ross. Objectivity in the eye of the beholder: divergent perceptions of bias in self versus others. Psychol Rev. 2004 Jul;111(3):781-99.

dynamics we operate within, that modern corporate life occurs against the backdrop of an epidemic of loneliness.

## Loneliness

One of the most pervasive but rarely discussed aspects of modern life is the ubiquity of loneliness. Whether arising from social media, the loss of connectivity associated with reduced religiosity, longer working hours, or decreased civic engagement, almost half of Americans report feeling lonely to some degree,[35] with one in five experiencing social isolation either "always or often."[36] This figure increases to one in three for adults over 45 years old.[37] Canada faces similar statistics, with 20% of men and 25% of women reporting feeling lonely at least weekly.[38] Loneliness is an epidemic, and with the workplace playing a central role in people's lives, it is only natural that they seek meaningful relationships with their colleagues.

If you pass a sea sponge through a sieve into a bucket, the individual creatures break apart and become separated in the

---

[35] Cigna. "Cigna U.S. Loneliness Index: Survey of 20,000 Americans Examining Behaviors Driving Loneliness in the United States," 2018.
[36] DiJulio, Bianca, Liz Hamel, Cailey Muñana, and Mollyann Brodie. "Loneliness and Social Isolation in the United States, the United Kingdom, and Japan: An International Survey." Henry J Kaiser Family Foundation, August 2018.
[37] Anderson, G. Oscar, and Colette Thayer. "Loneliness and Social Connections: A National Survey of Adults 45 and Older." AARP Research, 2018.
[38] Raina PS, C. Wolfson, S.A. Kirkland, L.E. Griffith, M. Oremus, C. Patterson, H. Tuokko, M. Penning, C.M. Balion, D. Hogan, A. Wister, H. Payette, H. Shannon, and K. Brazil. The Canadian longitudinal study on aging (CLSA). Can J Aging. 2009 Sep;28(3):221-9.

cloudy water. While they can survive independently, they instinctively seek each other out. After a couple of hours, they will have rebuilt their city. Humans have the same needs; the allure of independence, once realized, leads to mental and physical sickness, followed by the compulsion to reconnect.

All forms of social connectedness are in decline, including religiosity, community organizational membership, and invitations to homes.[39] This is an epidemic that affects everybody. For people, who are designed for community, the long-term impact of this crisis is still not known. Mammals in zoos without companionship lose interest in food, become listless, and stop sleeping.[40] Monkeys stop growing and develop heart disease if separated from their simian peers.[41] Babies without companionship and socialization do not survive.[42] We are built for community, and without it, we suffer greatly.

The loneliness that people experience at work impacts their performance[43] and, without genuine friendships, leads to a lack of trust and higher stress.[44] High quality personal connections,

---

[39] Putnam, Robert D. Bowling Alone: Revised and Updated: The Collapse and Revival of American Community. Simon & Schuster, 2020.

[40] Franklin, Jon. Molecules of the Mind: The Brave New Science of Molecular Psychology. Atheneum, 1987.

[41] Kaplan J.R., S.B. Manuck, T.B. Clarkson, F.M. Lusso, D.M. Taub, and E.W. Miller. Social stress and atherosclerosis in normocholesterolemic monkeys. Science. 1983 May 13;220(4598):733-5.

[42] M. T. Erickson. Child psychopathology : assessment, etiology, and treatment. Prentice-Hall, 1978.

[43] Ozcelik, Hakan, and Sigal G. Barsade. No Employee an Island: Workplace Loneliness and Job Performance. Academy of Management Journal 61, no. 6 (2018): 2343–66.

[44] Patel, Alok, and Stephanie Plowman. "The Increasing Importance of a Best Friend at Work." Gallup, 2022.

however, help organizations achieve their goals.[45] The quality of interpersonal relationships at work is more than a nice-to-have; it is a critical component of their engagement and impacts their ability to effectively collaborate. Relationships grounded in trust and fairness light up the reward center of the brain, releasing dopamine, leading to a positive feedback loop with increasing mutual trust and confidence, as well as positive attribution where the employees believe the best of each other.[46]

The assumption of positive intention is a requirement for reciprocal altruism. If we cannot assume that the other person has our interests at heart, we cannot work together in anything but the most transactional way. Without that, we would simply not have the ability to cooperate with strangers. The corollary is that when individuals experience feelings of isolation, the brain lights up as though the person is experiencing physical pain.[47]

If we look beyond the psychological, positive social interactions at work also positively impact the body's physiological processes. They improve the effectiveness of cardiovascular, immune, and neuroendocrine systems by reducing cardiovascular reactivity, stabilizing hormonal patterns, and strengthening the immune system.[48] These psychophysical benefits are

[45] Dutton, Jane, and Emily Heaphy. The Power of High Quality Connections. Barrett-Koehler, 2003.
[46] Geue, P. E. (2018). Positive Practices in the Workplace: Impact on Team Climate, Work Engagement, and Task Performance. The Journal of Applied Behavioral Science, 54(3), 272–301.
[47] Dunbar, Robin. Grooming, Gossip, and the Evolution of Language. Harvard University Press, 1998.
[48] Heaphy, E. D., & Dutton, J. E. (2008). Positive social interactions and the human body at work: Linking organizations and physiology. The Academy of Management Review, 33(1), 137–162.

material changes and support self-perceptions of well-being. Employees who report having social interactions in the workplace are also more likely to report having positive feelings about their work.[49]

In *Together*, author and physician Vivek Murthy relays a story of his early days in medicine when he was meeting with a patient named James. James was being treated for symptoms related to diabetes and seemed listless and depressed. With some prompting, he said that the worst thing that happened to him was when he won the lottery. He recounted the story of how he, previously a baker, thought a life of leisure and luxury would make him happier. He gave up his job and his daily contact with repeat customers and moved to a wealthier neighborhood. He lost touch with old friends and became isolated. He realized his mistake too late, saying, "I traded in my friends and a job I loved and moved to a neighborhood where people keep to themselves in their giant houses. It's lonely."[50]

Success in a technical role similarly leads to a reduction in human contact. Junior practitioners interact with many people as they are learning. However, as they develop into a specialist, they become increasingly distant from interacting with stakeholders. They find themselves several steps removed from the business case and equally detached from delivering the output to the requestor; project tracking software mediates all of their human relationships.

---

[49] Nolan, T. & Küpers, W. (2009). Organizational climate, organizational culture, and workplace relationships. In R. L. Morrison & S. L. Wright (Eds.), Friends and enemies in organizations (pp. 57–77). Palgrave Macmillan.
[50] Murthy, Vivek. Together: The Healing Power of Human Connection in a Sometimes Lonely World. Harper Wave, 2020.

Researchers have found that loneliness is typically associated with the absence of one of three crucial relationships. People need an intimate partner, quality friendships, and a network of peers who share their interests and sense of purpose.[51] Whether someone is introverted or extraverted, a certain level of fulfilment across all three dimensions is necessary for satisfaction.

While we cannot single-handedly fix the loneliness epidemic, recognizing its pervasiveness is crucial for recognizing the emotional state of most people. In our world, both peers and stakeholders are seeking more than just a paycheck and a promotion; they are starved for companionship and seeking meaningful partnerships.

Cognitive empathy requires only the ability to understand that others have their own mental states. We can use that knowledge to adjust our approach without any investment on our part. As we mature in our journey towards becoming more empathetic, we will find that genuine emotions arise.

## Emotional Empathy

In contrast to the more logical and depersonalized understanding involved with cognitive empathy, emotional empathy is sharing a genuine personal connection and mirroring the feelings of the other person.

Using the earlier example, if a friend tells us that they were turned down for a promotion at work, cognitive empathy will tell us that this person is likely sad and discouraged, and we

---

[51] Austin, B. A. (1983). Factorial Structure of the UCLA Loneliness Scale. Psychological Reports, 53(3), 883–889.

would likely try to alleviate their negative feelings. If we are particularly close to this person, we may experience emotional empathy, and feel personally affected. Our beneficence, or genuine desire for the other person's happiness leads us to authentically share in their frustration. Cognitive empathy drives us to action based on rational evaluation of the situation while emotional empathy drives us to action based on our own compassion.

If your life is based on your own projects and plans, what can your attitude be to those who are in your way? They are an annoyance whose random personal events get in the way of what you are trying to achieve. If your stance is one of love and empathy, though, you're not trying to get them out of your way; you are seeing their misfortune as an opportunity for kindness. Those with more developed emotional empathy wake up each day with a very different fundamental attitude. They are more oriented towards other people and try to find these opportunities for kindness.

Many would argue that this level of emotionality does not belong in the workplace; they believe we should make pragmatic decisions based on organizational goals. Some may concede that cognitive empathy is permissible to smooth over the unavoidable emotionality of their frailer peers but are unwilling to yield further ground. The reality is that humans have depth; they are physical, spiritual, and emotional beings. While they must temper personal desires and control their reptilian brain to collaborate and achieve objectives, denying the greater part of themselves can only lead to long-term personal dissatisfaction.

Our default orientation is to think socially. While debugging a SQL script, we may temporarily pause it, but as the non-analytical part of our brain turns off, the social part immediately lights up. When studied under an fMRI, researchers observe two distinct networks supporting social and non-social thinking. As one diminishes, the other comes online.[52] Enabling cognitive empathy requires intentional reflection and can be approached procedurally. On the other hand, enabling emotional empathy is more challenging, as it demands a reevaluation of what it means to be "professional".

Empathy should not be transactional. Bishop Robert Barron described that as an indirect egotism, where one is nice to another with the implicit expectation of reciprocal kindness. Fraternal love, the ideal we should aspire to, involves genuinely willing the good of the other and taking actions to bring it about. It is about getting out of the black hole of our egos.[53]

Navigating a relationship that is traditionally adversarial, such as with technology functions in many organizations, can be challenging. When we feel wronged, the instinct might be to seek revenge or find a way to vent our frustration. While it may seem logical that releasing this pressure would make us feel better, research suggests that it often leads to increased dislike for the other person. Bullies, for example, may experience cognitive dissonance after their actions, rationalizing by convincing themselves that the victim deserved mistreatment or that they were helping toughen them up. It's a reminder that few people perceive themselves as the "bad guy" in their own narrative.

In a study conducted by Michael Kahn, blood pressure

---

[52] Cook, Gareth. "Why We Are Wired to Connect." Scientific American, October 2023.
[53] Bishop Robert Barron. On the Holy Spirit. Wordonfire.org, 2012.

readings were taken from a group of students while Kahn behaved rudely towards them. Afterwards, one group of students had the chance to give feedback to Kahn's supervisor, whereas the control group was not. One would assume that those who could express their complaints would feel better, but the opposite was true. Expressing their anger prolonged their elevated blood pressure, and they harbored greater animosity towards Kahn. Alternatively, those who did not have the opportunity to vent quickly returned to normal.[54] We need to be more willing to turn the other cheek.

This effect can be used positively in reverse. When we perform favors for people, we end up seeing them in a more positive light. In an experiment by Jecker and Landy, groups of students who had participated in a paid study were divided into three groups. The first group was informed by the researcher that the study had run out of money, and the organizer was personally asking if they would return some of their payment. The second group was asked less personally by a secretary to return some of the money. The third group was not contacted and allowed to keep all their money. After some time, each group was asked about their impression of the researcher. Those who kept their money were neutral, as it was a transactional experience. Those who were asked by a third party to return money were soured on him because it was impersonal. However, those who he asked personally for money reported the highest opinion of him.[55] Even though the third group was

---

[54] Kahn, M. (1966). The physiology of catharsis. Journal of Personality and Social Psychology, 3(3), 278–286.

[55] Jecker, J., & Landy, D. (1969). Liking a person as a function of doing him a favour. Human Relations, 22(4), 371–378. See also the "Ben Franklin Effect", named for a recommendation by the statesman in his autobiography that a person ask for favors to establish friendly relations with difficult people.

financially worse off than the first, they had a higher opinion of the researcher solely because they had helped him. The person we helped must be a good person because we helped them, and we must be good people because we help good people.

We should not see these studies as life hacks or opportunities to exploit. Instead, they serve as reminders that we are happier when we make others happier. People are designed for community, and when we isolate ourselves or try to build dehumanized frameworks for our interactions, we are less satisfied and less productive. However, practicing mindfulness, embracing stress, and working towards the good of our stakeholders leads to deep personal fulfilment.

## Mindfulness

While the thought of mindfulness can suggest hip nonsectarian spiritualism, the practice exists across cultures by different names. Hindu and Buddhist traditions practice *sati*, a remembrance to observe. The Muslim tradition encourages the virtue of *muraqabah*, or attentiveness. Catholics have the *examen*. In the West, we tell our children to count to ten when they are angry, forcing them to take a moment for reflection. It appears all cultures have found their way to this concept of intentional presence, drawn in by the clear benefits.

Practicing mindfulness can increase focus,[56] boost your immune system,[57] reduce stress,[58] improve your memory,[59] make you more compassionate,[60] and more empathetic.[61] Being able to understand the perceptions of others improves your mental health[62] and makes you more popular.[63] There is overwhelming evidence of its ability to positively impact our mental and physical health.

---

[56] Kerr CE, Jones SR, Wan Q, Pritchett DL, Wasserman RH, Wexler A, Villanueva JJ, Shaw JR, Lazar SW, Kaptchuk TJ, Littenberg R, Hämäläinen MS, Moore CI. Effects of mindfulness meditation training on anticipatory alpha modulation in primary somatosensory cortex. Brain Research Bulletin. 2011 May 30;85(3-4):96-103.

[57] Davidson RJ, Kabat-Zinn J, Schumacher J, Rosenkranz M, Muller D, Santorelli SF, Urbanowski F, Harrington A, Bonus K, Sheridan JF. Alterations in brain and immune function produced by mindfulness meditation. Psychosomatic Medicine. 2003 Jul-Aug;65(4):564-70.

[58] Weinstein, N., Brown, K. W., & Ryan, R. M. (2009). A multi-method examination of the effects of mindfulness on stress attribution, coping, and emotional well-being. Journal of Research in Personality, 43(3), 374–385.

[59] Zeidan F, Johnson SK, Diamond BJ, David Z, Goolkasian P. Mindfulness meditation improves cognition: evidence of brief mental training. Conscious Cognition. 2010 Jun;19(2):597-605.

[60] Mascaro JS, Rilling JK, Tenzin Negi L, Raison CL. Compassion meditation enhances empathic accuracy and related neural activity. Soc Cogn Affect Neurosci. 2013 Jan;8(1):48-55.

[61] Schulte, Brigid. "Harvard Neuroscientist: Meditation Not Only Reduces Stress, Here's How It Changes Your Brain." Washington Post, May 26, 2015, sec. Inspired Life.

[62] Keltner, Dacher, Jason Marsh, and Jeremy Adam Smith. The Compassionate Instinct: The Science of Human Goodness. W. W. Norton & Company, 2010.

[63] Slaughter V, Imuta K, Peterson CC, Henry JD. Meta-Analysis of Theory of Mind and Peer Popularity in the Preschool and Early School Years. Child Dev. 2015 Jul;86(4):1159-1174.

The popular image of mindfulness is the yogi sitting cross-legged, serenely observing the passing world. That could not be more distant from the developer being asked, just this once, to deploy a change to production on a Friday afternoon. Asking a data engineer to take an hour to meditate when the sky is falling is a non-starter. Fortunately, even the smallest act of mindfulness can help. When a situation arises, we need to simply take a breath before acting.

The practice does not need to be exotic mysticism, and it does not require dedicated time. When we find ourselves in conflict with an angry stakeholder, take a breath and consider their perspective. When our servers go down, take a breath, and recall that this has happened before and will happen again. When we have a compilation error, take a breath, and anticipate the joy of finding the errant semicolon.

In the mid-2010s, the hot topic in Silicon Valley was microdosing. Developers were enhancing their creativity by ingesting small amounts of hallucinogenic mushrooms. They found that this practice gave them an edge in their careers and improved their enjoyment of their work. The use of mind-altering substances to boost creativity has been endorsed (with several caveats) by Joe Rogan, Scott Adams, and Steve Jobs.[64]

Others take small doses of MDMA, a psychoactive drug that induces a sense of emotional openness and love. Certainly, side effects like grinding teeth, paranoia, and hallucinations are not conducive to productivity. The goal of these drugs is to foster an altered state that makes the participant more mindful and empathetic, not to provide raw horsepower. Fortunately, one can achieve the same thing without resorting to illicit

---

[64] Kelly, Jack. "Silicon Valley Is Micro-Dosing 'Magic Mushrooms' To Boost Their Careers." Forbes, 2020.

means.

Mindfulness is a precursor to empathy. It's only once we move out of our own morbid frames and feelings and consider the bigger picture that we can appreciate our role. Also critical to that paradigm shift is adjusting our perception on stress.

## Embracing Stress

We want to believe that the human mind is born a blank slate, and that anything good or bad in our personality is due to influences by culture and rearing. In the 17th century the prevailing idea was humanism. In the 19th century it revolved around the tension between Marxism and capitalism. Today, the dominant force is the struggle between progressivism and conservatism. It's a comforting thought that society molds us in a particular way, and that we possess free will within those boundaries. Regrettably, this is a fantasy; genetics plays a major role in our behavior, and there is a limit to have far we can deviate from our biology.[65] We do not wield as much control as we imagine. Nevertheless, with maturity and self-awareness, we can flex our frontal cortex enough to moderate our base instincts.

As instinctual creatures, we have a natural inclination to enhance our comfort. We construct houses for safety, cultivate and store food to reduce hunger, and install a mini-fridge by our workstation to reduce unnecessary walking. We take all reasonable steps to alleviate stress through avoidance or mitigation. Both pursuits are natural and good; they are animating forces in our lives. However, if we were to achieve the goals of

---

[65] Pinker, Steven. The Blank Slate: The Modern Denial of Human Nature. Penguin, 2003.

infinite comfort and zero stress, the impact would be disastrous.

We desire free time, but a life devoid of meaningful work would be meaningless. Recoiling from stressful interactions, we are tempted towards submission, and avoid competition justifying it by some higher philosophy. Unfortunately, the only way to opt out of competition and reduce stress is to assume the lowest possible position on the pecking order. At this point, there is no autonomy; the stronger will be making decisions for the meek. We redefine losing as success and find countless victories afterward. The more we submit, the more submissiveness becomes acceptable to us.[66]

As we seek the comfort of having others make decisions for us, we decline in social standing, and become physically disfigured. Animals undergo a remarkable transformation as they descend in position, eventually coming to look the part. Monkeys at the bottom of their hierarchy, for example, exhibit stooped shoulders and passive mannerisms. For a human, being respected and having influence reduces blood pressure, prevents mental decay, and lessens the risk of stroke.[67] People in higher positions also have higher levels of testosterone and fewer stress hormones.[68] While the desire to seek comfort and reduce stress is compelling, achieving this is horrible for our health

---

[66] Jackson, W.M. Why do winners keep winning?. Behavioral Ecology and Sociobiology 28, 271–276 (1991).
[67] Tomoshok, Lydia, Craig Van Dyke, and Leonard S. Zegans, Emotions in Health and Illness: Theoretical and Research Foundations, Lond: Grune & Stratton, 1983. see also Bower, Bruce. "Chronic Hypertension May Shrink Brain", Science News, 12 September 1992.
[68] Sapolsky, Robert M. Lessons of the Serengeti: Why some of us are more susceptible to stress, The Sciences, May/June 1988, 42.

and well-being.

When primates succeed or achieve a higher status, they receive a boost of serotonin.[69] There is a key difference for humans, however. While chimps can only receive this benefit as individuals, we can abstract our peer recognition to our in-group (e.g., religion, country, or business function).[70] Being part of a winning group makes us feel like winners individually, and physically we respond the same way.

Choosing passivity also reduces our ability to think creatively and be the source of organizational innovation that we are meant to be. In addition to the social norms that are established, it makes us fearful to experiment. People that are in danger or under chronic stress are biologically driven to be more conservative. Birds, when well fed, are more adventurous in what they eat, while those who are starved or stressed will only eat what they are familiar with.[71] This behavior can also be seen at a macro level. Faced with electrification, the British Empire clung to traditional manufacturing. Despite the clear rise of digital photography, Kodak stuck with tradition. Blockbuster confidently advertised its rental experience while Netflix ate their breakfast. When we are under threat, whether real or imagined, we find it challenging to innovate.

We also seek to reduce stress by limiting the time we spend working. When we advocate for work-life balance, we need to be mindful of what the "life" side of the hyphen represents.

---

[69] Frank, Robert H. Choosing the Right Pond: Human Behavior and the Quest for Status. Oxford University Press, 1985.
[70] Fukuyama, Francis. "Identity, Immigration, and Liberal Democracy". Journal of Democracy 17, no. 2 (April 2006): 5-20.
[71] Morse, Douglass H. Behavioral Mechanisms in Ecology. Harvard University Press, 1982.

The opposite of work is not life, but idleness. The opposite of life is not work, but death. We should aspire instead to an integrated life, where we balance our familial responsibilities, our community involvement, and our vocational endeavors. Rather than trying to avoid stress, we should look to embrace it as an essential part of our lives.

Periods of acute stress are necessary and encourage growth. When we present to a group of stakeholders or when we choose to challenge somebody in a meeting, we are going through the same chemical experience as our lion-fighting forebears. The alternative is avoidance, which turns our healthy acute stress into a long-term chronic stress, leading to physical and emotional decay.[72]

G.K. Chesterton, when traveling the United States in 1981, commented with great admiration that Americans tended to discuss their work and aspirations while the British discussed their leisure. It is a symptom of a culture in decline that focuses on relaxation above accomplishment.[73]

We should aspire to have a healthy relationship with stress and work and strive to instill this mindset in those we care about.[74] Work plays a crucial and, perhaps, unparalleled psychological role in shaping self-esteem, identity, and a sense of order.[75] Our aim as leaders should be to foster challenging yet

---

[72] Taleb, Nassim. Antifragile: Things that gain from disorder. Random House, 2012.
[73] Chesterton, G.K. What I saw in America. Anthem Press, 2009. Originally published as a series of essays in 1922.
[74] Selye, H. Stress without Distress. In: Serban, G. (eds) Psychopathology of Human Adaptation. Springer, 1976.
[75] U.S. Department of Health, Education, and Welfare. Work In America: Report of a Special Task Force to the U.S. Department of Health, Education, and Welfare. The MIT Press, 1973.

supportive environments where individuals can develop in character and capability, rather than simply eliminating stress.

## Compassion

As people experience the vices and predations of the modern world, they are rarely able or willing to make room for the needs of others. While we may grasp at a theoretical level that those we interact with harbor their own motivations and goals, employing cognitive empathy enables us to imaginatively place ourselves in their position and adjust our actions accordingly.

We may also experience an emotional response to the challenges faced by others. When we see our colleagues grappling with anxiety, we may, in turn, feel a sense of anxiousness through emotional empathy. However, it is when both our cognitive and affective empathy drive us to act, propelling us to go out of our way to alleviate the suffering of others, that we are said to be demonstrating compassion.

It is clearly not enough to just perceive and understand the emotional states of others. If we open ourselves to this and do nothing, we will take on their burden without any benefit. We need to intentionally decide to make a change in how we approach others if we are going to realize the benefits of empathy, and to share them with others.

When we are part of a group, whether at work or elsewhere, we tend to wait and hope that a situation will resolve itself. In group settings, bystanders are less likely to intervene, assuming that someone else will step in. This diffusion of responsibility results in people choosing not to take ownership, leading to inaction.[76] Remember, the standards we walk past are the standards that we accept. It is crucial to take ownership of situations and help our peers. While it may be uncomfortable, in most cases, bystanders will rally to support us. Empathy without action is masochism.

## Compassion Fatigue

Acting in the service of others is an admirable trait, but we need to remain aware of our own limited capacity and make time for self-care. When we are encumbered with professional responsibilities shouldering the additional weight of others' emotional well-being, there is risk of becoming overwhelmed.

Compassion fatigue is the process where empathy decreases as the number of people one cares for increases. Over time, individuals may not only care less but actively resent those who burden them emotionally. Like in an airplane, we must put on our own masks before helping others.

We need to be mindful not to take on too much. Starting small, aiming to help people in our direct periphery, and expanding over time can alleviate this. We also need to be cautious not to conflate empathy with niceness. Sentimentality and untethered niceness can ruin a person and a team more quickly than their absence. In willing the ultimate good for a person, we often must deny them.

---

[76] Keltner, Dacher, Jason Marsh, and Jeremy Adam Smith. The Compassionate Instinct: The Science of Human Goodness. W. W. Norton & Company, 2010.

## Five Tips for Being Empathetic

The science behind empathy is interesting, but without application, it's ultimately meaningless. If empathy without compassion is masochism, theory without action is sadism. The following activities can enable and support an empathetic geek, but they should not be viewed as simple assignments that will provide immediate benefit.

Being empathetic cannot be seen as a one-and-done project. It is an adjustment to our internal mechanisms, a redefinition of professionalism, and a personal commitment to seeking the good of the other. Deconstructing this into five simple tips risks oversimplifying what is a lifelong pursuit.

Geeks, armed with the theory and immediate takeaways, can establish a foundation for future development. Adopting empathy as a guiding principle, rather than a mere framework, is crucial to realizing its full effect.

### 1. Positive attribution

Attribution is the process of inferring the cause of events or behaviors. Whether consciously or not, we engage in this practice every day, both reflecting on our own lives and observing others. When looking outward, we rarely do so with charity.

When we are late for a meeting, we have knowledge of all the preceding events: our children forgot their mittens, we caught every red light, the daycare was disorganized, and our access card didn't work; everything was outside of our control, justifying our tardiness. However, when somebody else is late for a meeting with us, we see it as a lack of conscientiousness, a sign of disrespect, and a personal slight that mars our perception of them.

This actor-observer asymmetry is well-documented. It is a natural bias that leads us to blame external forces for our own situations, but personal failings when the same situation befalls other people. Because we have much more information about our own condition, we are better able to explain it. However, because all we have from the other person is what they tell us, we tend to assume the worst. The original proponents of this theory, Jones and Nisbett, more succinctly stated, "actors tend to attribute the causes of their behavior to stimuli inherent in the situation, while observers tend to attribute behavior to stable dispositions of the actor."[77]

The actor-observer bias is a specific form of attributional bias that has a significant role in how we perceive and interact with each other. It holds no value for either the observer or the actor. Our natural inclination to assume the worst in others has a negative impact on everybody involved.

When we intentionally choose to assume the best about other people, we practice positive attribution. We give the recipient the same leeway that we allow ourselves and we feel better as a result. In fact, a study of attributional styles among nurses found that "[...] the more positive one's occupational attributional style, the more likely one is to use problem solving and positive cognitive restructuring strategies and the less likely one is to use avoidance strategies to deal with workplace stress." Leveraging these optimistic explanatory styles is linked

---

[77] Jones, E. E., & Nisbett, R. E. (1987). The actor and the observer: Divergent perceptions of the causes of behavior. In E. E. Jones, D. E. Kanouse, H. H. Kelley, R. E. Nisbett, S. Valins, & B. Weiner (Eds.), Attribution: Perceiving the causes of behavior (pp. 79–94). Lawrence Erlbaum Associates, Inc.

with positive mood, better perseverance, higher levels of achievement, and overall well-being. Negative attribution, meanwhile, is linked with feelings of hopelessness, depressive symptoms, and lower self-esteem.[78]

Negative attribution also arises within team settings. We tend to remember events in a way that overestimates our own contributions and underestimates the contributions of others. For example, when husbands and wives are asked about how much of the housework they do, wives on average say they do 90% of the work while husbands claim 40%. These ratios may change depending on the relationship, but in all cases the sum of their contributions exceeds 100%.[79] This distortion over time helps us to believe our own lies, and eventually to remove our own sense of accountability for past failures.

Always assume the best intentions of each person that you are working with. Regardless of whether you agree with their decision or not, everybody makes the choice they feel that is best with the information that they have. It warrants being explicit – nobody sets out to be the bad guy, and nobody is actively trying to derail the work of others. In cases where it seems that there is an overt attempt at sabotage, explore their motivations more deeply. What appears superficially to be pure malice is likely a deeper unexplored distrust of some aspect of the project.

---

[78] Peterson, Christopher, and Tracy Sheen. Optimistic Explanatory Style. The Oxford Handbook of Positive Psychology, 3rd, ed., 2019.

[79] Ross, M., and Sicoly, F. (1979). Egocentric biases in availability and attribution. Journal of Personality and Social Psychology, 37(3), 322–336.) see also Thompson, S. C., & Kelley, H. H. (1981). Judgments of responsibility for activities in close relationships. Journal of Personality and Social Psychology, 41(3), 469–477.

Instead of seeing detractors as obstacles with a vendetta, seek to understand and practice positive attribution. Even if they remain detractors at the end of the exercise, the geek will be better off personally by assuming the best.

## 2. Take time for active reflection

Between sprint planning, backlog maintenance, stakeholder meetings, and time devoted to real work, there is always something vying for our attention. Our productivity tools alert us that our calendar is too full, and kindly offer to schedule some time for focus. We consider and wearily decline. The thought of committing 20 minutes a day to idleness while watching our inbox grow is anxiety-inducing.

Career and life coaches have long recommended reflection, journaling, and mindfulness to enhance our quality of life and improve work performance. We know that it works. We install apps to remind us to breath and focus, make New Year commitments, and start bullet journals, but they end up propping our monitors.

Most technology workers are hard-wired to be tactical, linear thinkers who can set an objective and execute against it. We start to solution problems before stakeholders have even finished describing them. Generic active reflection techniques and designated focus time, lacking tangible output, are in complete opposition to the mechanics we use in our daily work.

Active reflection and mindfulness shouldn't be confined to specific, discrete times spent in quiet meditation but rather integrated as a step in our checklist for everything we do.

Before and after each interaction, we need to be deliberate in considering the individuals and their positions. When people surprise us with a peculiar question, we should not jump to a substantive answer, but look beneath the query. We should take two seconds to mentally put ourselves in their situation and answer the question, "under what circumstances would I be asking this question?"

If one of our team members is requesting additional training, consider the motivations behind the request. Before delving into the budget and engaging the Learning and Development team, take a moment to reflect. Is it consistent with past behavior? Is it paired with performance issues, or a lack of engagement? Have one of their peers recently received a new certification and they feel the need keep pace? Are they feeling stagnant in their career? It's important to recognize that seeking additional training is often motivated by more than a simple desire for knowledge. Reflect on the individual, the context of the request, and strive to understand the underlying reasons beyond the surface-level ask.

Likewise, when a stakeholder asks whether we have considered a certain tool or platform, take the time to actively reflect on their motivations. If the person asking is not normally technically proficient, it is worthwhile to investigate the source of their information. While the proposal may be impractical, outright dismissal does more than reject the idea – it is a rejection of the requestor. Our mental map should include the person and the request, not solely the technology.

Recognize that, in their mind, they are not asking us to completely re-factor our code and processes to fit a new technology. It is likely that they do not fully understand the implications of their suggestion. Their motivation might extend beyond a technical understanding – perhaps they're trying to build a relationship by expressing interest in our domain. It's possible that they have come across an article or heard discussions elsewhere. They might even have acquaintances with a specific vendor and want to offer them support. Take the time to see the person behind the ask.

Most of us lack the time in our day to carve out specific time for focus and reflection, but we all have the time to think before responding. Being deliberate about active reflection does not need to be onerous. When properly integrated into our daily conversations and activities, it becomes a time-saving tool that fosters stronger, more empathetic relationships.

Incorporate intentional reflection before and after each interaction and integrate it into your personal checklist for projects.

### 3. Get real feedback

Honest conversations are difficult. Everybody has been part of an annual performance review where they are praised as exceptional, only to receive a "meets expectation" score. Bold practitioners seek ways to achieve the elusive "exceeds expectations" rating, only to watch their leader abdicate responsibility, citing arcane policies.

For those tasked with providing feedback, the temptation to hide behind policy can be great. Offering honest feedback exposes the reviewer. Laying out the ways where the employee falls short may lead to a discouraged and disengaged employee, or, more dangerously, a formal complaint about fairness. The path of least resistance and lowest risk is redirection.

The risk of candor so greatly outweighs the benefits that even with reassurances the counterparty will be hesitant to honestly engage. This anxiety surrounding direct feedback from leaders will likely not change in the foreseeable future. Asking subordinates for feedback puts them in an equally challenging position. Fearing repercussions, they will claim to be absolutely delighted with their manager right until their colorful exit interview.

However, the inclination to minimize responsibility can be strategically leveraged to gather authentic feedback. Once a relationship has been established, instead of directly asking for their feedback, inquire about what they are hearing about you.

Giving the other person the clear opportunity to reduce conflict by reframing their feedback as coming from somebody else will improve the quality and quantity of feedback that you are receiving. Pre-empt their next concern, that you are going to ask them where it is coming from, by saying you want it to be anonymous.

Asking somebody to provide an opinion about your work performance is a high conflict question that most, regardless of their feelings, will avoid. However, asking somebody what they are hearing from others about your work performance, is a much lower-risk question.

Feedback is crucial for improving performance and relationships within organizations. Framing questions empathetically will elicit authentic feedback, and responding maturely to this feedback is instrumental in personal and professional growth.

### 4. Start small

In the 1990s, British anthropologist Robin Dunbar asserted that there was a cognitive limit to the number of individuals that a person could maintain relationships with. Based on the

ratio between different primate brain sizes and their typical social circles, Dunbar suggested that a human could only maintain a relationship with 100 to 250 people.[80]

Building on this concept, Jason Pargin coined the term
"monkeysphere" to describe the number of people that a person can typically empathize with.[81] For someone living in a city
of several million, tossing a broken cup into their garbage involves little thought. Garbage collectors in a city are anonymous. In contrast, a resident of a small town might take extra
care, bundling broken glass to ensure the garbageman's safety.
Our capacity to care about others reaches a limit before emotional exhaustion sets in. If we cared for each of the eight bil-
lion people in the world equally, we would be bedridden with
worry.

To avoid empathy fatigue, we cannot abruptly shift our focus from the technical landscape of our workplaces to the personal well-being of all stakeholders and clients. We must start
small to effect impactful change, learning to triage and differentiate. By intentionally selecting who is included in our monkeysphere, we can maximize our impact without facing
burnout.

The work of the technology function has a daily impact on
all members of an organization. Whether in delivery, networking, security, business intelligence, or development, we are discussed (and often cursed) around dinner tables. Though it

---

[80] Dunbar, R, 1992, Neocortex size as a constraint on group size in
primates, Journal of Human Evolution, 1992, v22, 469-493
[81] Pargin, Jason. "What Is the Monkeysphere?" Cracked, September 30, 2007. https://www.cracked.com/article_14990_what-mon-
keysphere.html. Originally published under the pen name David
Wong.

would be an untenable emotional burden to take that personally, we should embed empathy into our processes and seek to understand the human impact of our work. Sociologist Richard Sennett emphasizes that the simple act of collaboration can "join people who have separate or conflicting interests, who do not feel good about each other, who are unequal, or who simply do not understand one another."[82] Finding balance and starting small are key to maintaining a healthy and empathetic relationship with our colleagues.

### 5. Exercise your heart

Few technology workers entered their fields because they had a deep connection with the human experience. If they did, their life would have taken them down more people-centric career paths. Generally, it is the cold determinism and sense of control that brought us into this profession. When our code didn't compile, it was due to incorrect bracket nesting, not an arbitrary subjective decision by the compiler (usually).

If our predisposition, training, and workflows conspired to bring us to this point, and all training and development serve to continually reinforce our logical thinking, it can be a struggle to pull out of that style of thinking. It is important to look for opportunities to exercise the creative and empathetic side of our character to maintain a balanced personality.

There is nothing more human than storytelling, but our genres tend toward the fantastical. When interstellar conflict and elemental assassins form the backdrop of our fiction, it

---

[82] Sennett, Richard. Together: The Rituals, Pleasures, and Politics of Cooperation. Yale University Press, 2013.

mutes the human element. The beautiful complexity of our re-lationships is lost. Reading broadly can help us to become more empathetic and well-rounded people, in particular those stories that elevates the ordinary and expand our moral imagination.

Volunteering our time to non-profits and social groups that we otherwise might not have exposure to is another way to expand our emotional vocabulary. Look for organizations that have exposure to wide-ranging social issues such as Rotary or other community groups.

Finally, take time for self-reflection in the form of prayer or meditation to tune in to yourself. When you become familiar to your own signals, you naturally become better at identifying them in others.[83]

There is an expression by Goldsmith Marshall that what got you here will not get you there. If we stick within our routines and consume only the media that aligns with our views, we will not be able to understand other perspectives as much as if we made a conscious effort to expand our thinking. As much as we exercise our bodies and our technical abilities, we need to work to exercise our hearts.

## Summary

It is a wonderful paradox that the main benefits of empathy lie with the person sharing it. We are social creatures, ordered towards community and mutual service. When we live and act

---

[83] Murthy, Vivek. Together: The Healing Power of Human Connection in a Sometimes Lonely World. Harper Wave, 2020.

within the framework we are designed for, we will find our-selves happier, healthier, and more resilient to the challenges that we will face. The empathetic geek is not just a more valu-able employee – he or she is a happier and more self-actualized person.

People are predisposed towards goodness, and towards ser-vice. Adam Smith said, in a quote that deserves to be replayed in full, "Nature, when she formed man for society, endowed him with an original desire to please, and an original aversion to offend his brethren. She taught him to feel pleasure in their favorable, and pain in their unfavorable regard. She rendered their approbation most flattering and most agreeable to him for its own sake; and their disapprobation most mortifying and most offensive would not alone have rendered him fit for that society for which he was made. Nature, accordingly, has en-dowed him, not only with a desire of being approved of, but with a desire of being what ought to be approved of; or of being what he himself approves of in other men. The first de-sire could only have made him wish to appear to be fit for so-ciety."

Many technology workers have, through rejection by others or inborn introversion, purposely decided live apart from oth-ers, seeing social integration as a binary. Accepting the anxiety that comes from living in contradiction to Smith's first rule, they plant their flag and tolerate the personal consequences.

Smith went on to say, "The second was necessary in order to render him anxious to be really fit. The first could only have prompted him to the affectation of virtue, and to the conceal-ment of vice. The second was necessary in order to inspire him with the real love of virtue, and with the real abhorrence of vice. In every well-formed mind this second desire seems to be

the strongest of the two. It is only the weakest and most superficial of mankind who can be much delighted with that
praise which they themselves know to be altogether unmerited.
A weak man may sometimes be pleased with it, but a wise man
rejects it upon all occasions. But, though a wise man feels little
pleasure from praise where he knows there is no praise-wor-
thiness, he often feels the highest in doing what he knows to
be praise-worthy, though he knows equally well that no praise
is ever to be bestowed upon it. To obtain the approbation of
mankind, where no approbation is due, can never be an object
of any importance to him. To obtain that approbation where it
is really due, may sometimes be an object of no great importance to him. But to be that thing which deserves approbation, must always be an object of the highest."[84] If we, by our
natural introverted predispositions, can accept being on the
outskirts of social circles, we cannot simultaneously be enthusiastically offensive.

We are not fooling anybody by doubling down on our
aloofness. C.S. Lewis wrote, "a proud man is always looking
down on things and people; and, of course, as long as you are
looking down, you cannot see something that is above you."[85]
Geeks may not be the life of the party, but we should still show
up.

When we recuse ourselves from society, personally or professionally, we lose sight of the bigger picture. We can no
longer put our lives and activities into context, and we lose the
opportunities for the deep personal satisfaction that comes
from helping others. When we pursue the benefit of others, we
should seek "no purpose in friendship save the deepening of

---

[84] Smith, Adam. The Theory of Moral Sentiments. Cambridge University Press, 2012. Originally published in 1759.
[85] Lewis, C.S. Mere Christianity. Harper San Francisco, 2023.

the spirit. For love that seeks aught but the disclosure of its own mystery is not love but a net cast forth: and only the unprofitable is caught."[86]

Making the choice to live artificially, where we ignore the human elements of our lives, will not benefit us in the long run. Technology, oriented towards elevating human dignity, is a great good. As the people responsible for delivering the benefits of this technology, we have a hand in bringing joy to the people within our lives. If we measure that benefit by utilitarian metrics, in the end, their joy is not diminished, only our own.

However, we still need to accept that people, with noble intentions, may oppose our work. Worse still, they may see us, as the human face of the technology, as their personal adversaries. We need to remember that people are naturally fearful of change and will attack the person they see as the change agent to ease their pain and restore their perception of order. They are not attacking us as people; they are trying to escape what we represent. We should not retaliate against the individual but, out of respect to the person, seek to understand their position. We must deescalate the situation and not retaliate by managing our environment and vulnerabilities.[87] When our workplaces are full of confrontational people, our days are full of anxiety and worry. We need to reframe our thinking and see the organization instead as a place of competing ideas.

Regardless of political bent, few people could resist the charisma of Bill Clinton. Even among Republicans, he was almost universally liked. He had what seemed to be a natural charm.

---

[86] Gibran, Kahlil. The Prophet. Alfred A. Knopf, 1973. Originally published in 1923.
[87] Heifetz, Ronald, and Marty Linsky. "A Survival Guide for Leaders." Harvard Business Review, June 2002.

Though his abilities may have looked like a natural gift, he was privately very methodical. Clinton would put all the information that he had about people on index cards. As he learned more about the person, he would fill up the card, edit it, and annotate it. His collection eventually grew to 10,000 cards before he had them digitized. It took all his life to collect those physical artifacts of the relationships he built. His seemingly effortless charm was built on a practiced intentionality about building relationships.[88] No amount of natural charisma can compete with a person who puts a lifetime of effort into building and maintaining a network.

You need self-control to be able to order yourself towards others. It is not asceticism or blind altruism, but a commitment to direct your gifts towards helping others. It is not just a path to greater productivity and professional success, but it is a path to greater personal happiness.

---

[88] Holiday, Ryan. Ego is the Enemy. Portfolio, 2016.

# LEVERAGING EMPATHY

*"I've told you this a dozen times and I don't know how much clearer I can be. That data will never reconcile to accounting. The next time they ask you to investigate an outage please just tell them, 'No'"*

*"I know we've been over it, but this is going to keep coming up. You know how to fix it, what do you need? What will it take? This is a distraction, and I can't get anything else done."*

*"I've tried for years, and I've given up. Just tell them to hire somebody else to fix it or to stop asking."*

Every technology worker has experienced situations in which leaders underestimate the difficulty of completing a task. When estimates of the level of effort are shared, they scoff and reject the project, only to return the following month, questioning why it hasn't been completed. This cycle inevitably leads to more comprehensive project plans, increased efforts to explain, and heightened mutual frustration, with little or no progress achieved.

*"I appreciate you walking me through the reasons why it doesn't line up with accounting, but I need it fixed. This keeps coming up and we need*

*a solution or a way to quickly say why it is out."*

*"My understanding is that this was started years ago and just wasn't finished. The job started in the early 2000s and your predecessor's predecessor said it was close enough, my predecessor agreed, and unfortunately, we've inherited that decision."*

*"My concern is today and there is zero justification for the numbers coming out of my stack to be wrong every month."*

Mark Twain said that, to a man with a hammer, everything looks like a nail. When posed with the same question, a UX researcher, a data scientist, and a management consultant may respectively respond with user interviews, a decision tree, and an operating model. Without zooming out to comprehend the situation fully, there's a risk of answering the question heard rather than the one that was asked.

Organizations with siloed functions lacking mutual intelligibility will suffer false starts, rework, and frazzled nerves, as people struggle to understand and support each other. The organization's overarching goal may become obscured as people advocate for their own agendas and build their own fiefdoms.

When a business leader and a technology leader are trying to understand each other, there are only two alternatives. Either the business leader must learn enough about the geek's world to be able to clearly articulate their needs, or the geek needs to put aside their instinctual apathy and seek to understand their stakeholder.

*"Just to confirm what I'm hearing, are we okay to keep using this data if we can make you a tool that explains the variance?"*

*"Yes of course, it doesn't need to be exact. I just can't keep getting sidelined in meetings and having no backup."*

To maximize the impact within our organizations, we need to avoid solutioning until we have understood the problem. Rather than asking our users to provide a problem statement so we can begin our independent exploration, we need to ask the users where they want to be and find the shortest path to get there. We can never accomplish this without empathy.

Leaders must instill empathy in their reports, and organizations need to encourage empathetic thinking in their leaders. In the situation described, the underlying issue was not a technical challenge, but a miscommunication. When the business leader said that he wanted to know why the data was wrong, the data team heard that leadership wanted the data to be correct. When the data team said they needed a year to resolve, the business leader felt he was being dismissed, as he expected a straightforward answer to his simple question.

*"I just got out of a meeting with the boss — your dashboard saved him; it showed where the outage was, and he was able to move right along. He's really impressed with the team because of what you made."*

*"I spent five years making business cases for re-engineering the warehouse to make the data right — wish he would have told me he just wanted a spreadsheet."*

When we complete a new type of project, or hit a new peak in our career, we can look back over the meandering path we took and reflect that if we had better information at the time, we could have achieved our goals in a fraction of the time. It is easy to see what a person should have done after a situation has resolved itself. We share this universal truth between ourselves after a project is completed and ultimately, we learn nothing.

We will never have perfect information, but we do have the ability to sit, listen, and learn before jumping in. In this scenario five years were spent in frustration, several rejected project plans were created, executives spent hours reconciling numbers, engagement suffered, and the data team stagnated due to a perceived lack of skill. Potentially hundreds of thousands of dollars in misallocated resources, all for want of a spreadsheet that took four hours to create.

At the heart of this scenario is a lack of understanding; we do not share a common language with our stakeholders. Calvin wrote that, "language is the expression of the mind, as it is commonly said, and it is therefore the bond of society. Had there been no language, in what would men differ from brute beasts? One would barbarously treat another; there would indeed be no humanity among them."[89] We cannot collaborate without speaking the same language.

When working in isolation, we do not see how extreme the differences are. The small variations in expressions, rules, manners, expectations, that make up our different subcultures only become apparent when we see them violated during an exchange with somebody outside of our group. If we cannot effectively communicate with the people we aim to serve, we cannot expect them to adapt. We need to be the ones to adjust.

The empathetic geek is not only happier and more pleasant to work with; he or she is able to create more value in their organizations. The era of technology workers relegated to a backroom function has passed. Best-in-class organizations are leveraging the unique skillset of these workers and including them in all facets of business operations. This shift does not demand technical depth; rather, it requires an intentional cultivation of empathy.

---

[89] Calvin, John. Commentaries on the Prophet Jeremiah and the Lamentations, vol. 9.

## Generational Differences

After a relationship matures it becomes much easier to empathize with a person. Battles fought together build comradery and mutual trust, creating fertile ground for further collaboration. However, when people work together for the first time, there is often a long process of getting to know each other and establishing team dynamics. The "forming, storming, norming, performing" model proposed by Tuckman lays out well the friction that may precede each project. [90]

Finding one's place in any new team or project is made more difficult by the fact that most people adopt a veneer of professionalism that needs to be worn down before authentic relationships can be formed. Hints of humanity from colleagues and mutual respect eventually erode these artifices. Like dating, we need to spend enough time together before the real personalities emerge.

Approaching these interactions with an open mind is challenging, especially as a participant under the sway of the same cultural mores. Adopting an objective and systematic lens, and purposefully seeking to understand the other people involved, can smooth the forming stage, reduce the storming, and move more quickly to performing.

To be empathetic we need to understand the perspective of the other person, and a big part of that is understanding the factors that influence their perspective. Upbringing, cultural characteristics, and childhood fears all influence people in adulthood. While making broad brush assumptions about an individual based on any categorization, including age, is unwarranted, considering generational characteristics can serve as a

---

[90] Tuckman, Bruce W (1965). "Developmental sequence in small groups". Psychological Bulletin. 63 (6): 384–399.

useful starting point. Lived experiences shared among these generational categories help us begin to establish an understanding.

These differences are compounded by the complexity of the social dynamics between the people involved. Genuine communication can only happen between peers. Those above you have a moral claim to their status and no motivation to accept corrections. If they are exposed as wrong, they risk losing status. Those below you lack the necessary context, could be motivated by spite, or are influenced by position. Peers only need to be convinced. Outside of this, we all have our defaults; younger generations approach baby boomers from a place of naïveté, while a Gen Xer approaches a Gen Zer from a place of authority.

These generational differences should only be a first step, reinforced or abandoned based on technical posture and organizational context. These categorizations also have limited applicability outside of the West and can vary by country. People need to be willing to quickly adjust or abandon in consideration of personal characteristics that become apparent.

We need to recognize that we are working with individuals, not groups. The emphasis should be on developing personal with individuals rather than relying on a collective. Freud said groups are "impulsive, changeable, and irritable" and "led almost exclusively by the unconscious."[91] Understanding the individual motivations lets us ensure that decisions are made before we sit down to formalize.

---

[91] Freud, S. Group psychology and the analysis of the ego. Boni and Liveright, 1922.

## Baby Boomers

This large demographic cohort succeeded the silent generation, with individuals born between 1945 and 1965, marking the post-war baby boom. They grew up in a time of great economic prosperity[92] and have a markedly higher IQ than the preceding generation.[93] The baby boomers, owing to substantial post-war government subsidies, was the most highly educated generation in history. During their youth they witnessed continual economic growth and maintained left-leaning political views until the mid-1970s.

Now, in the twilight of their careers, the majority of baby boomers have largely reverted to the traditional family values of their parents. They support fiscal constraint as their retirements approach.[94] Despite demographers warning of a talent crunch in preceding decades as boomers were expected to leave the workforce, a larger number than expected have delayed their retirement.[95]

The COVID-19 pandemic has somewhat paused this trend, prompting many to take an unplanned retirement.[96] As of

---

[92] Jones, Landon Y. "How 'Baby Boomers' Took over the World." Washington Post, November 6, 2015, sec. Opinion.

[93] Baker, D.P., Eslinger, P.J., Benavides, M., Peters, E.; Dieckmann, N.F., & Leon, J. (2015). The cognitive impact of the education revolution: A possible cause of the Flynn Effect on population IQ. Intelligence, 49, 144-158.

[94] Saad, Lydia. "U.S. Still Leans Conservative, but Liberals Keep Recent Gains." Gallup, January 8, 2019, sec. Politics.

[95] Fry, Richard. "Baby Boomers are staying in the labor force at rates not seen in generations for people their age". Pew Research Center, 2019.

[96] Cassella, Megan. "The Labor Shortage Will Get Worse and May Last for Decades." Barron's, September 2, 2022.

2017, boomers constituted 25% of the workforce[97] and, being in the latter stages of their careers, are heavily represented in senior and executive leadership positions.

Boomers are highly ambitious and work-centric people. Having begun their careers during a period of sustained economic stability, many have achieved financial independence. Despite this, they continue to prioritize monetary rewards as a motivational factor, alongside a desire for peer recognition. Perks such as parking spaces, job titles, and respect for their experience hold significant importance to them.

Shaped by a career spent in a culture that rewarded corporate loyalty, they, in turn, expect loyalty from others. The proclivity for job hopping exhibited by younger generations makes boomers inherently distrustful; they look for loyalty, duty, and teamwork in their reports. They believe that individuals need to make sacrifices to be successful, and that achievement comes after paying one's dues.[98]

Success in one's work naturally leads to a reduction in risk-taking. In the early stages of a person's career, there is little to lose by stretching and taking risks. However, as one gathers esteem and accomplishments, the fear of reputational damage discourages risk-taking, resulting in tepid incrementalism.

The notion that work should be a source of personal satisfaction is a relatively modern concept that gained traction later in the lives of this generation. John Burnett, after conducting interviews with 18th century workers, observed that "for most, work was taken as a given, like life itself, to be endured rather

---

[97] Fry, Richard. "Millennials are the largest generation in the U.S. labor force." Pew Research Centre, 2018.
[98] Rampton, John. "Different Motivation for Different Generations of Workers." Inc, 2017.

than enjoyed; most were probably glad enough to have it at all, and to expect to derive satisfaction or happiness from it was an irrelevant consideration."[99]

During the 1960s and 1970s, younger, better-educated, and more affluent workers began to see work as a source of self-respect and a means to experience personal fulfilment.[100] Boomers are the last generation to have the perspective that work should not necessarily be enjoyed but suffered with dignity. Therefore, attempting to appeal to their anticipated need for self-actualization can backfire, as it may seem selfish and contrary to their values.

Baby boomers typically operate under the belief that all is well unless informed otherwise and do not feel the need for daily check-ins. In contrast to younger generations who value continuous feedback and frequent interactions with their leaders, the boomer perspective interprets these check-ins as a lack of trust in their abilities.

The technical posture of this cohort varies significantly, perhaps more than any other. However, it is crucial to highlight that for functional specialists within a business unit, they are often operating within a paradigm that they themselves instituted. Consequently, efforts to change that paradigm can be seen as a personal affront, and recommendations lacking a deep understanding of the conditions that led to that process can be quickly dismissed. Technology workers need to show respect to the existing process and genuinely seek to understand the limitations and constraints that the stakeholder was

---

[99] Burnett, John. Useful Toil: Autobiographies of Working People from the 1820s to the 1920s. Psychology Press, 1974.
[100] Kanter, Rosabeth. Work in a New America, Daedalus: Journal of the American Academy of Arts and Sciences, 1978.

under.

If recommendations lack a clear business context, the technology proposed may be summarily dismissed. In David Brooks' *The Second Mountain*, he illustrates life's course as navigating two mountains. The first represents worldly pursuits, as a person achieves prestige, professional success, and popularity. However, upon reaching the summit, a realization dawns that there is another mountain behind it – one of purpose.[101] In the latter part of one's career, you need to know that it all meant something, and that your work was important.

Most boomers are looking at that second mountain at the same time that geeks are seeking to upend the processes they created. Some respond positively, seeing it as evolution in which they played a part. Some face it with dread that their work was ultimately meaningless.

Younger boomers, with only a few years until retirement, are reluctant to invest their remaining time learning new tools and approaches. There is a deep fear of losing relevance[102] and seeing their life's work supplanted by somebody who has not paid their dues or struggled enough to earn their respect. Understanding this emotional state is key to removing barriers.

The mischaracterization of boomers as obsolete, spoiled, and self-absorbed, is a toxic idea that has derailed many projects. Dismissing their concerns is rejecting decades of practical experience. While it is true that often this generation delivers

---

[101] Brooks, David. The Second Mountain: The Quest for a Moral Life. Random House, 2019.
[102] Haserot, Phyllis Weiss. "The Biggest Work Fears of Boomers, Gen Xers and Millennials." nextavenue, March 20, 2018.

their feedback in a way that younger geeks could see as aggressive, we always need to see it as coming from a place of genuine caring for their department and organization.

Baby boomers represent a wealth of information and continue to carry significant influence in organizations. Respecting their experience, asking their advice, and seeking their mentorship are key to fostering a productive working relationship and personal advancement.

What to do:

• Keep it professional. Unless initiated by them, concentrate on building rapport through benign topics such as weather and traffic. While younger generations often consider personal questions a show of caring, for baby boomers, it can be regarded as immature prying into their personal lives.

• Learn from their experience. In a rapidly changing field where specific capabilities can quickly become outdated, understanding of people and processes is timeless.

What not to do:

• Thank them. Show appreciation for their time, celebrate the quality of their work, but do not directly thank them for performing their job. Boomers see work a source of meaning and dignity, and expressing gratitude for meeting expectations may convey an underestimation of their talents.

• Force check-ins. This cohort generally does not seek the same level of emotional and social support as younger generations, and a daily check-in will almost always be interpreted as a lack of confidence in their abilities. In established Agile organizations this can be reinforced by being cautious about prying too deeply into their activities and trusting that they will raise alarms when necessary.

## Generation X

This cohort includes people born between 1965 and 1980 to silent generation and early baby boomer parents. Often lost between the more plentiful and vocal boomers and millennials, this generation has a distinct culture and set of values focused on independence and authenticity.

During a period marked by the social liberation of the baby boomers, which resulted in higher divorce rates and increased female labor participation, Gen X were often left to fend for themselves. Referred to as "latchkey-kids" they often returned home to an empty house and had to unlock the door themselves with a hidden key. This early need for self-reliance and lack of parental supervision instilled an inherent independence that has persisted throughout their lives.

Further contributing to this experience was the societal shift during their youth, where a lesser emphasis was placed on children. Children were regarded as secondary to the self-actualization and happiness of the parents.[103] They were described as being "the first group to grow up without a large adult presence, with both parents working."[104] This circumstance led to Gen X being more peer-oriented than previous generations.

This generation witnessed the era of *laissez-fair* economics under Reagan, general neoliberal policies, the fall of the Berlin Wall, Watergate, and the collapse of the Soviet Union. The right-wing political environment that emerged as a response to the threat of communism dissipated during their youth, leading most at the time to be nominally liberal but not particularly

---

[103] Howe, Neil, and William Strauss. 13th Gen: Abort, Retry, Ignore, Fail? Vintage, 1993.
[104] Corry, John. "A Look at Schools in U.S." The New York Times, September 4, 1984.

politically active. Rather than advocating for a specific position, they were generally apolitical and were indifferent to global affairs. Experiencing a lack of stability, both at home and in public institutions, and witnessing their parents' hard work without reaping the corresponding benefits, Generation X developed a preoccupation with authenticity and a strong aversion to "selling out."

They were also the first generation to have personal computers in their homes and at school.[105] Without parental supervision or a strong sense of community, many immersed themselves in technology. In their early to mid-careers, those who eventually entered the technology space found themselves in an environment of great optimism. They experienced the first liberal government of their lives under Bill Clinton and witnessed a large drop in unemployment in the US.[106] Fueled by their independence, technical acumen, and distaste for corporate life, many were motivated to start their own companies, constituting the highest percentage of startup founders at 55%.[107] Unfortunately, this shift from being perceived as cynical slackers to entrepreneurial heroes was quickly quashed by the early 2000s dot-com crash. They spent the next decade in the wilderness before technology regained its footing and financiers returned to the space ready to invest.

Now, in their mid to late careers, they are "savvy, skeptical and self-reliant; they're not into preening or pampering, and

---

[105] McCrindle, Mark. "The Generation Map". McCrindle Research, 2019.

[106] Amadeo, Kimberley. "President Bill Clinton's Economic Policies." The Balance, 2020.

[107] Rampton, John. "Different Motivations for Different Generations of Workers: Boomers, Gen-X, Millennials, and Gen-Z." Inc., October 17, 2017.

they just might not give much of a hoot what others think of them. Or whether others think of them at all."[108] They have also shifted firmly towards conservatism, surpassing even the boomers and the silent generation in how quickly they have moved to the political right as they age. Having lived and worked through the dot-com crash, the global financial crisis, and the pandemic, they harbor distrust for interventions by governments, employers, or political lobbyists. Their lived experiences have shaped a libertarian philosophy that there are no handouts, nobody is going to help you, and when institutions get involved, it is usually for the worse.[109]

They are motivated by personal and professional interests above the interests of the company and will move on quickly if their employer will not meet their needs. They are also resistant to change if it impacts their personal life. Now parents and grandparents, they, better than anyone, understand the emotional consequences of their absence and prioritize their own families, holding them in higher regard than past cohorts.[110]

In *Generation X*, the book that named the generation, Douglas Coupland writes, "[…] portraits emerge, those of fanatically independent individuals, pathologically ambivalent about the future and brimming with unsatisfied longings for permanence, for love, and for their own home." He goes on to write, "I was both thrilled and flattered and achieved no small thrill

---

[108] Taylor, Paul, and George Gao. "Generation X: America's Neglected 'Middle Child.'" Pew Research Center, June 5, 2014.
[109] Ramanathan, Lavanya. "We Thought Gen X Was a Bunch of Slackers. Now They're the Suits." Washington Post, March 1, 2017, sec. Style.
[110] Nulsen, Charise Rohm. "A Look at the Different Generations and How They Parent." FamilyEducation, 2023.

of power to think that most manufacturers of life-style accessories in the Western world considered me their most desirable target market. But at the slightest provocation I'd have been willing to apologize for my working life – how I work from eight till five [...] performing abstract tasks that indirectly enslaved the Third World."[111]

The slackers have become the suits, now occupying just over half of leadership positions globally. Perhaps due to their youthful ambitions of "not selling out", they tend not to advocate for themselves as vigorously as boomers and millennials, resulting in a slower progression in their careers compared to either group.[112] This moderated professional development has afforded them more time to cultivate relationships and to enhance their leadership abilities. They are adept at leveraging their network and are strong collaborators.

Though they are not as eager to dismantle established practices and institutions as millennials, they are more pragmatic than baby boomers. They tend not to be as attached to process or organizational history and are willing to discard old processes if they can be convinced, based on technical merits, that the new approach is superior. However, it is important to articulate the risks and mitigations to build credibility and demonstrate thorough consideration of potential issues.

Except for the oldest Gen Xers, this cohort is digitally native. They are completely comfortable using social media, general desktop applications, and home automation software,

---

[111] Coupland, Douglas. Generation X: Tales for an Accelerated Culture. St. Martins Griffin, 1991.
[112] Neal, Stephanie, and Richard Wellins. "Generation X — Not Millennials — Is Changing the Nature of Work." CNBC, April 11, 2018.

taking pride in their technical savviness. This pride can some-times lead them to dismiss newer technologies as they grapple with the cognitive dissonance of no longer being the technical experts. Helping their aging parents set up Alexa has given many of them an unjustified sense of their technical acumen, and anything that diminishes that can be seen as passing fad not worth understanding. They tend not to adopt new technology without a compelling use case and are less motivated by novelty when compared to their younger colleagues.

It is important with this group to create points of comfort within a project by leveraging skeuomorphs. Maintaining an ornamental version of what was a functional necessity in an older approach can provide a sense of stability and continuity, reducing the stress of a completely revamped approach. Providing details around risk mitigation can also help lower barriers. Before doing so, it is particularly important to understand the individual level of understanding for people in this cohort.

As reports, they have a high degree of autonomy and prefer to be given objectives with the freedom to accomplish them in whatever way they see fit. As leaders, they view providing the same level of autonomy to their reports as a sign of respect. However, this is complicated by the fact that autonomy is also their default when stakeholders are not technically sophisticated enough to suggest an approach. In practice, this means that a Gen X stakeholder may provide business requirements but have a desired approach in mind that they withhold out of respect. Misinterpreting this as ignorance can lead to a perceived slight by either party.

The nonverbal communication is further complicated by the lack of formality among this cohort. Gen X is generally more casual than baby boomers, which, when contrasted with other senior leaders, can create a false impression of apathy.[113] Taken together, a Gen X leader providing vague requirements in a seemingly disinterested way can be a display of great respect. The same behavior, if coming from a baby boomer, would be a sign of great indifference.

These highly technical, independent, emotionally complex, and aloof leaders are often overlooked in discussions around generational differences. However, their unique characteristics and over-representation among technology leaders make it valuable to understand their idiosyncrasies. Their executive ascendancy in light of boomer retirement, combined with their focus on networking and collaboration, will demand greater attention in the future.

What to do:

• Ask for details. When collaborating with this group, they often withhold detailed requirements out of respect, potentially leading to unnecessary iterations. Directly inquiring for more information will not only yield greater insights but will also be seen as a display of passion.

• Give autonomy. The corollary to the request for details is their preference for the respect of a loosely defined outcome, assuming they can provide their own detail. During scoping or planning exercises, provide the milestones and key requirements, and work together to establish the connecting pieces.

What not to do:

• Patronize. This cohort values directness and may misinterpret excessive niceties as a lack of urgency. Feedback

---

[113] Indeed. "What Is Generation X?" Indeed, 2022.

should be respectful but direct, and timelines need to be explicitly stated.

- Be bureaucratic. Process, without a clear benefit, is stifling for this cohort. Any policies or workarounds should be framed as enablement rather than control.

## Millennials

This cohort has been blamed for the death of bar soap,[114] the diamond industry,[115] and cereal,[116] as well as more material concerns such as the economy and manufacturing. Much has been written about this group, and most of it is negative. Now approaching middle age, most millennials tend to shrug off these curious attacks. Representing 35% of the workforce and gradually filling the void left by retiring baby boomers, they stand as the most heavily represented cohort in the workplace.[117]

Their reputation for being idealistic dreamers who struggle with adulting was not entirely undeserved in their youth. As they have matured, however, their idealism has evolved into a more formally principled stance. Their persistent questioning of the status quo has made them innovative, providing a different perspective than previous generations. Increases in a corporate focus on equity and environmentalism in the late 2000s likely would not have found the necessary support in

[114] Picchi, Aimee. "Blame millennials for the vanishing of bar soap." CBS News: Money Watch, August 25, 2016.
[115] Fraser, Kristopher. "Why Have Millennials Fallen Out of Love With Diamonds?" Daily Beast, April 13, 2017.
[116] Fox News, Are Millennials Cereal Killers?, May 2, 2023, On Air.
[117] Fry, Richard. "Millennials are the largest generation in the U.S. labor force." Pew Research Center, 2018.

world dominated by only Gen X and boomers.

The need for affirmation, work-life balance, and expectations for advancement have all contributed to a narrative that seeks to infantilize this generation. Millennials lived through events such as September 11th, the war on terror, frequent school shootings, the global financial crisis, and Hurricane Katrina. They also experienced a surge in income inequality, with the costs of housing and education skyrocketing compared to older generations. Witnessing a deteriorating world against the backdrop of their hardworking parents who ferried them between extracurriculars activities, they questioned what was truly important to them.

They then began their careers in an economy where, for most, no amount of work could provide them a traditional lifestyle. This reality was cemented during the 2008 global financial crisis as they saw their parents lose their homes and jobs. Consequently, they now have little trust in financial institutions and believe everything is ephemeral.[118]

The reputation for being high maintenance and needing constant feedback and affirmation is a negative portrayal of what is an achievement-oriented group seeking constant challenge and growth. Their desire to be known personally and managed by their results, which spurs their need for immediate feedback, shows an unrecognized passion for their work.

However, they are also the first generation that believes work should be enjoyed rather than endured. They actively seek roles that offer substantial vacation time and are willing to leave organizations where they sense a misalignment of val-

---

[118] Anonymous Contributor. How the 2008 Financial Crisis Affected the Millennial Generation, FiscalTiger, December 10, 2019.

ues. They aspire to work for organizations that foster innovative thinking, develop their skills, and make a positive contribution to society.[119] This inclination can frustrate senior leaders who, after deciding on an approach, find the project challenged on some perceived irrelevant bases, such as fairness or equity.

For older cohorts, having millennial peers means they cannot outright dismiss these concerns. Employing positive attribution and realizing that a holistic view of projects is critical can help to find wisdom in these challenging interjections. Corporate millennials represent the voice of the largest market,[120] and organizations that do not appeal to millennials will suffer. Gen Z, who are even more socially conscious, are 50 years removed from most senior leaders. The bridging perspective that millennials provide is critical to fostering meaningful discussions in this area.

Managing this cohort, especially for a Gen X leader, can be perplexing. The respect that autonomy on technical approach implies is regularly misinterpreted. Millennials are often guilty of confusing latitude with freedom. While these freedoms, parochial as they are, may start as a positive, over the long term, they can lead to disengagement as they struggle for direction. In response, more senior leaders lose confidence, and resort to ever greater micromanagement, and the relationship spirals towards an exit.

The millennial stakeholder can seem indifferent in the beginning of a project. This continues during planning, where

---

[119] Deloitte. "Big demands and high expectations: the Deloitte millennial survey." Deloitte, 2014.
[120] Fromm, Jeff. "As Gen Z's Buying Power Grows, Businesses Must Adapt Their Marketing." Forbes, 2022.

they often let others guide the conversation. However, this disinterest is rarely aimed at the project but is a lack of concern for the status quo and a higher tolerance for risk. While older generations would deeply interrogate the new solution to ensure its readiness for deployment, millennials are quite comfortable with change. With in-flight projects, millennials jump comfortably between the details and overarching project metrics, showcasing their adaptability as project managers.

Creative and socially conscious, this cohort will inevitably reshape the way organizations operate as they move into positions of influence. Without a nuanced understanding of their motivations, a business-oriented pragmatist may appeal to principles that do not align with their values, struggling to make a meaningful connection. Properly nurtured relationships with millennials can contribute to a broader professional network, and, given the strong ethical standards they hold, acceptance on professional terms becomes a proxy for personal endorsement. The *realpolitik* that can be expected from others is absent in this group. If they accept you, they will promote and affirm you across their network.

What to do:

• Provide a rationale. Merely instructing this cohort on what needs to be done is insufficient; they require an understanding of the motivations behind the tasks and a clear vision of the future state, emphasizing human factors. Without a sense of meaning in their work, they are often prone to disengagement.

• Be personal. Hard work is not a path to self-respect for a millennial. They crave personal thanks and individual recognition. It is the sense of accomplishment and contribution to a team effort holds value for them.

What not to do:

• Be overtly political. Technology practitioners can never entirely shy away from politics; however, an explicit quid pro quo with a millennial will be poorly received and leave a negative impression. Instead, discuss the greater good and extend favors without an explicit expectation for reciprocation.

• Celebrate busyness. When we recognize our peers for their overtime, or flaunt our 70-hour workweeks, we sent an implicit message that time-on-post is the path to success. To align with the values of this cohort, we need to celebrate impact and effort rather than emphasizing the amount of time spent.

## Generation Z

Born between 1997 and 2012, this generational cohort is just beginning to enter the workforce. While their personalities are still developing, they seem to represent a natural evolution of millennials, with the most unique feature being a focus on work-life integration rather than work-life balance. Unlike previous generations that sought to protect their personal lives from the office, Gen Z weaves them in a way that is baffling to their colleagues. Texting their team at 2am on a Saturday, taking an unplanned vacation day on a Wednesday, and openly discussing their family problems in a team meeting, they can appear erratic.

This is even more apparent for managers of this group. They want daily feedback and consistent recognition, wanting to feel that their boss is also their friend.[121] Daily standups that

---

[121] CGK. "How to Easily Engage Gen Z Employees in the Workplace." Centre for Generational Kinetics, 2018.

address only the progress of projects are a personal affront to Gen Z, who wants to be asked about their feelings. It is not sufficient for them to collaborate on a project; they want to know about your personal life.

This group came of age during the global financial crises, had access to technology from birth, and grew up in a climate of extreme independence where there were few limits or cultural pressures to conform to any standards. They are the least literate, and when they do read, it tends to be superficial material they can consume in a few minutes.[122] Most of their content consumption happens on social media, with very few preferring long-form articles.

Gen Z output is much like their input. Often, in the stilted style of their rapid-fire TikTok videos, they will erratically message the group channel with ideas, observations, good-natured gossip, personal reflections, bits of code for peer review, and memes.

Senior leaders, believing that Gen Z has not yet proven themselves, will assign a single activity to work on, then wait for that to be completed before assigning the next. This serial approach to work, well-suited to Gen X and boomer leaders, is impossibly repressive to a Gen Z, who are not just adept at multitasking but whose internal wiring demands it.

Because this is such a departure for most older leaders, Gen Z tends to prefer millennial managers whose working style, though not quite as manic, better matches their own. In a departure from the millennial cohort, this group is less likely to pursue opportunities in smaller organizations, with over half preferring to work for large companies. This is a big change

---

[122] Kowalczyk, Ola. "Which Generation Reads the Most?", ebookfriendly, July 28, 2020.

after years of decline. Older generations preferred the autonomy of smaller firms, but Gen Z are interested in the personal development they feel the larger organizations can offer.

They are also supremely flexible, with 75% willing to relocate, and 58% considering it acceptable to work evenings and weekends. However, this flexibility is not in addition to core working hours, it is in lieu of it. Gen Z expect reciprocity in their working lives and needs flexible work arrangements.[123] You can ask them to work until 2 am for a critical project, but you cannot expect them to be at the office during core hours.

Boomers expected, at a minimum, to be at the office from 9 to 5, Monday through Friday. They prided themselves on being the first to arrive and the last to leave, attempting to outwork their peers to show their commitment. Millennials would assess their total hours worked for the week and be satisfied if it was close to target, provided their objectives were being met. Gen Z can evaluate their workload over months, happily alternating between a ten-hour workweek and an 80-hour workweek to meet the current needs.

However, work isn't the most important thing for this group. They prioritize their wellness and time with their family. Like their millennial predecessors, they view work as something that should be personally rewarding and enjoyable, rather than merely tolerated.

After just beginning their careers, many were impacted by the pandemic, experiencing furloughs or layoffs. After nearly two years of seclusion and self-discovery, the people that returned to work are not the same as those who left. More than half of Gen Z workers in Canada are considering leaving their

---

[123] Lyons, Mary, Katherine Lavelle, and David Smith. "Gen Z Rising." Accenture, 2017.

jobs[124] after having tasted true workplace flexibility. Given the freedom to pursue their own hobbies, supported by stimulus cheques, and spurred on by an upbringing focused on equality over ability, they attach little of their self-worth to their work, instead focusing on their leisure activities. Sometimes, this stems from a lack of self-esteem, and at other times, from such a surplus that they wallow in it and abstain from all competitive activity.

It is impossible to motivate someone to greater achievement in the workplace with the promise of increased responsibility if they do not value work. Despite being recognized as the smartest and most self-assured generation, they are also the most self-centered, depressed, and stressed.[125] Changes in parenting methods for this generation have resulted in a more fragile mindset.[126] They are less equipped to deal with conflict, discomfort, or competition, and will casually resign if they have two consecutive bad days.

Unfortunately, for some in this group, corporate life is viewed as the source of ecological and economic scourges, and their employment relationship is one of necessity. They have little concern for the company's objectives. There are many who monkey-wrench on moral grounds in a quiet revolt against the machine and cannot be moved from their convic-

---

[124] Wells, Victoria. "The Great Resignation Isn't over yet: Workers Say They'll Quit If They Don't Get the Flexibility They Want." Financial Post, March 18, 2022, sec. FP Work.

[125] Borba, Michele. UnSelfie: Why Empathetic Kids Succeed in Our All-About-Me World. Touchstone, 2017.

[126] Lukianoff, Greg, and Jonathan Haidt. The Coddling of the American Mind: How Good Intentions and Bad Ideas Are Setting Up a Generation for Failure. Penguin Press, 2018.

tions. When pressed, they will happily move to the next organization, waiting patiently for the fall of capitalism to free them from their bondage.

It remains to be seen how this cohort will influence corporate life as they mature personally and advance in their careers. Negative characterizations of them as flippant and superficial may obscure their strengths in multitasking and raw productive ability. With time and experience, this group may well introduce a new method of work, one better suited to modern times than the traditional approach. Dismissing them outright, like any group, is a disservice to all involved.

What to do:

• Provide creative freedom. This cohort can become actively disengaged without the opportunity for personal expression, or if they feel like an underappreciated appendage of the machine. Provide a desired outcome, give the rationale, ideate with them, and let them lead the execution.

• Give deadlines. In the absence of time constraints, this generation tends to polish and experiment. With little commercial motivation, they are satisfied with endless churn. It is important to remind them often of deadlines and give them a safe opportunity to experience the consequences of failure and unmet deadlines.

What not to do:

• Leave them alone. The respect this represents for older generations is interpreted as disinterest with Gen Z, and without regular check-ins they may miss deadlines. Daily or even twice-daily touchpoints can help keep them on track and show that they have support.

• Underestimate them. In an environment of trust and

105

support, they can thrive and become highly productive. Conflating their need for emotional support with a lack of ability can lead to ongoing infantilization that will not allow them to grow and share their full capabilities.

## Technical Posture

As with generational considerations, it is helpful to understand the techno-emotional posture of your stakeholders. The approach to selling an idea to a person that is excited by new technology is much different than somebody who is a closeted Luddite, and the deeper the understanding of the stakeholder, the better positioned the geek is to meet their needs.

These categories are borrowed from Geoffrey Moore's seminal *Crossing the Chasm*,[127] where he describes four groups of customers based on their technological enthusiasm and risk appetite. This technical affinity can be gathered through conversation, reputation, or by discussion with their peers and reports.

It should be recalled that only individuals have a technical posture, and that functions and teams are comprised of several individuals. Innovators reporting to a late adopter may be able to convince their skeptical boss, but a group of primarily late adopters will need a different approach.

We should aspire to understand people individually, not to assume based on their role, age, or function. Taken in combination with generational differences and organizational context, the intersection of these categories provides a conceptual model for developing a change management strategy tailored

---

[127] Moore, Geoffrey. Crossing the Chasm. Harper Business, 2014.

to the stakeholder. However, it must be taken only as a starting point.

## Innovator

People who are innovators pursue technology for its own sake and want to interact with the newest tools and approaches. They are willing to accept risks, are fine with failure, and have little expectations for stability or quality. As techno-optimists, they value change and can quickly visualize how they will use it. They are excitable and will happily champion initiatives in which they see value.

It is trivial to convince this group to try a new approach, but critical that the focus is on painting a compelling vision of the future where, because of their faith, they get to share in the rewards. Presenting risk mitigation, connecting it to legacy processes, and illustrating how it is a natural evolutionary step diminishes excitement.

Innovators are natural risk-takers and expect something in return for that. Once a product reaches a point of stability where the majority begins to adopt it, they need to be able to say they were there first. This group gets excited seeing their name attached to projects and needs to be included in any project updates or marketing material. Personal callouts in group settings, attributing credit for supporting debugging, and letting them see deliverables before anybody else all titillate and keep people from this group engaged.

Many Gen Z fit into this category, with 78% reporting that

they feel AI and automation will enrich their working life.[128] Being new to the workforce, they have little connection to existing processes and feel no loss in replacing them with newer approaches. Finding champions within stakeholder groups is key to promoting adoption, and often, getting younger Gen Z team members excited about a project can wear them down from within.

The other side of their excitement of new things is their fickleness. They do not have the endurance to endorse a multi-year project because, before it is complete, a new technology will capture their attention. When something is new, it has their undivided attention, but that does not last long. Their new phone will end up in a shoebox before the warranty expires.

Ultimately, innovators are never abundant enough to provide the support needed for transformational projects. As individuals, their propensity for gambling is such that most churn out of companies through visible failures or a lack of risk management, and their proportion in senior levels is limited. For those who do reach senior levels in an organization it is usually survivorship bias, and with time they have more to lose and become more conservative.

The youthful energy of innovators is addictive, and though organizationally there may be hesitation in following them down a path, as individuals they often have more influence than their peers. Winning the support of an innovator should not be the last step, but it is a good first step, as they will be an outspoken champion for whatever initiative they support.

What to do:

---

[128] Lyons, Mary, Katherine Lavelle, and David Smith. "Gen Z Rising." Accenture, 2017.

• Let them leave their mark. Seek their advice throughout and incorporate a feature that they can point to, providing them a sense of ownership.

• Let them see under the hood. Polished final projects are dull to this group; they are excited by their exclusive access to beta products.

What not to do:

• Forget them. Keep them involved in the process and offer glimpses of future phases of a project. Their need for change means they can quickly find a new shiny object and lose interest in a project.

• Rest on them. While their energy is infectious, their support alone is not sufficient to provide the momentum larger initiatives require.

### Early Adopter

Individuals from this group are crucial to systematically pursue for project support. Early adopters possess most of the positive attributes of innovators combined with a higher degree of influence, both within the organization and in the broader industry. They are often considered thought leaders in their space and seen as people who know what the future is going to bring. Their reasoned approach, experience, and access to new technologies make them highly respected and a critical partner for any geek.

While innovators appreciate new technology for its own sake and pursue it independently once pointed towards something novel, this group is more focused on presenting themselves as being in the know. Innovators find joy in innovation, while early adopters find joy in being thought of as innovators. One practical consequence of this difference is that they require a lot more information, which they will seek out independently to be as objective as possible. They will want to review multiple sources, confer with their peers, look at competing products or philosophies, and work to get themselves to a level of understanding. Throughout this process they will provide feedback, have questions, and challenge your assumptions.

Early adopters see themselves as changemakers, and advocating for an approach or technology that does not gain traction is a personal failure for them. They will require more effort to get onside than innovators, but they will be far more powerful evangelists, as they put their reputation at stake when they vouch for something.

Getting support for a new project or technology from this group requires a different approach then innovators. Rather than focusing on the novelty of the product itself, or the impact that it could have to a narrow use case, we need to focus on how it impacts the industry or function. Frame the discussion around secular changes that support adoption of the product, competing organizations that are using or evaluating it, and provide articles that discuss it. Present opportunities, implicitly or explicitly, to turn a proof of concept into a prospective eminence building opportunity for the stakeholder personally. Support their self-perception as a change-maker rather than an incrementalist.

These individuals are rarely long-tenured or in senior leadership roles. Their focus on personal development and eminence demands that they have broad cross-industry experience, and as such, likely move between organizations frequently. They may be in senior individual contributor positions, hold strategic roles, or be on contract. One commonality is that their level of access and influence far exceeds what would be expected for somebody at their level. Investing in relationships with this group pays dividends over time.

Organizational support and adoption for technology initiatives depends on strong champions outside of the technology function. Innovators and technology workers, though certainly respected, do not have the necessary objectivity. Early adopters who are perceived inwardly and outwardly as being visionaries in their industry or function have the organizational influence to advance a project.

The rationality of early adopters can be frustrating, especially after the easy enthusiasm of innovators, but investing in gaining their support is necessary to convince the rest of the organization.

What to do:

• Understand their motivations. Early adopters are personally invested in their function and industry and need to be seen as the expert. Craft a narrative focusing on the big picture implications of the solution, not an incremental improvement to process.

• Discuss alternatives and risks openly. They will conduct significant research on their own and need to see you as a source of candid information. If they cannot trust you, they will find sources where you have no visibility.

What not to do:

• Dumb it down. Clumsy analogies make it look like you do not understand the technology yourself. They are often technically sophisticated, and if they are not, they will bring themselves to a conversational level.

• Share needless details. Unless asked, maintain laser focus on the value proposition for a product and what differentiates it from the alternatives.

## Early Majority

In *Crossing the Chasm*, it is the shift in priorities and motivations between early adopters and the early majority that is so different and challenging that it came to represent the titular gap. This concept is not new; in the 1962 book, *Diffusion of Innovations*,[129] author Everett Rogers outlined the spread of ideas and technology, illustrating how the niche appeal of innovators and early adopters gains self-sustaining momentum once the early majority embraces it.

The challenge becomes immediately clear when geeks try to convince early majority stakeholders to adopt a new approach. Often, technology workers use the same tactics employed with early adopters and innovators: framing the exercise as an exciting opportunity to try something novel and highlighting disruptive qualities for the industry. The chasm between these cohorts stems from this motivational misconception and the realization that novelty is a deterrent for most people.

Humans have evolved to be distrustful of new things. For our ancestors, encountering new animals could mean facing predators, new plants might be poisonous, and new locales posed a risk of getting lost. Those ancestors who were drawn

---

[129] Rogers, Everett. Diffusion of Innovations. Free Press, 2003. Originally published in 1962.

to novelty often faced unfortunate fates – being eaten, poisoned, or some other sad demise. Fortunately, their anxious homebody siblings lived long enough to produce us, their risk averse progeny.

Rather than emphasizing the originality of a solution, we need to highlight its impact on the organization and the improvement it brings to our stakeholders' quality of life. Reframing the project as an evolutionary step and establishing procedural connections between the old and the new can reduce discomfort. Incorporating skeuomorphs and ensuring a low-friction transition can encourage traditionalists to overcome their hesitations and embrace the change.

When selling ideas to early adopters and innovators, we try to embed buzzwords, we razzle dazzle, and try to generate excitement. It is a strategy designed to maximize stimulation and elicit a reaction. However, when dealing with the early majority, a shift in approach is needed. The focus should now be on reducing risk and building trust.

Rather than being perceived as an instigator of discomfort, adopt a role as a sympathetic guide, helping them navigate through the change. At the same time, we should not assume we know more about them than we do, and certainly not claim an understanding of their work. Approach these interactions with a quiet humility and authenticity; the majority will not become evangelists based on silly attempts to mimic them.

Once the early majority is on board, they can become powerful champions. Once people have mentally committed to a particular path, they will take all steps to reinforce that it was the right path to take. We are hard-wired to reduce cognitive dissonance, in particular when we have made an irrevocable decision.

In an illustrative behavioral study, it was found that people in a lineup to make a bet at a horse-track were less certain than those who had made their bets. The act of placing the bet and committing to an irreversible decision compelled them to feel with more certainty that they were right, despite no objective change in the probabilities of success.[130] To secure their long-term commitment, gain their buy-in, and encourage them to publicly declare it.

No initiative can be a success until the early majority cohort accepts it. While it might be disheartening after the ease and excitement of dealing with more change-positive stakeholders, the key to project success lies in understanding how to reframe opportunities to align with the needs of this group.

What to do:

• Bring your champions. As the instigator of change, your objectivity will always be questioned. Wherever possible, include innovators and early adopters in the conversation. People in the early majority tend trust their peers in the business more than technology workers.

• Tweak the narrative. While previous cohorts are excited by new technology and being on the cutting edge, this cohort is turned off by novelty. What might excite others discourages this group. Frame the solution as being a quality-of-life improvement that has been thoroughly tested, not as a new invention.

---

[130] Knox, R. E., & Inkster, J. A. (1968). Postdecision dissonance at post time. Journal of Personality and Social Psychology, 8(4, Pt.1), 319–323

What not to do:

• Take them for granted. Early adopters and innovators alone do not provide the numbers or the sensibility needed to take a change initiative to completion. Gaining and maintaining support among this group is vital for overall success.

• Lose momentum. Previous groups only needed to be shown the path, but this group needs to be walked the entire way. Leaving them at any point prior to their declared commitment will see them revert to legacy processes.

## Late Majority

This group is naturally skeptical of new products and will not be open to adoption until they are satisfied that others have sorted through all the bugs. They do not think in terms of product lifecycles and feel no need to follow trends. They make rational decisions based on their perceived risk-adjusted value. Without external forces, they would never independently adopt. They will only consider a change if the current approach is either eliminated or so inconvenient that it outweighs their desire for stability.

Because of this lack of intrinsic motivation to change, the previous approach of framing in terms of quality-of-life improvements will not work. It is more important for this group to hear stories about how others have adopted it, being very transparent about the challenges faced and how they were overcome. Hiding issues that arose to smooth over the process will have the opposite effect, causing worry that the bugs have not yet revealed themselves.

Often, geeks will conflate technological conservatism with technological ignorance. We should never assume that this group is populated with Luddites. Quite often, they can be technically sophisticated but, by disposition or professional necessity, want to be certain before adopting a new process or technology. Warren Buffet famously used a flip phone until 2020, despite owning over 5% of Apple.[131] Despite being clearly knowledgeable and having a collection of phones given to him personally by Tim Cook, he delayed his adoption of smart phones by 20 years and claims that he still uses it just "as a phone."

One of the fears within this group is not being able to roll back a decision. Explaining migrations, cutovers, points where they can opt out, all give a sense of control and reduce perceived risk.[132] Redesigning opportunities to embed future optionality can also help to alleviate their concerns.

The alternative always exists to pursue a mandated implementation from leadership. While it should not be the first step, there are situations where people cannot be convinced and need to be told. If an honest effort has been made, seeking executive support can help provide the final push. Regardless of the approach, during a larger migration project, it is important to be sure that they do not continue to use the legacy process until the cutover. This group often needs to be monitored to ensure that they are using new solutions during parallel phases.

At this stage in the transformation process, it can be exhausting to be challenged by a group of skeptical holdouts. The excitement of the early adopters and innovators has given way

---

[131] Valinsky, Jordan. "Warren Buffet finally traded in his flip phone for an iPhone." CNN Business, February 24, 2020.
[132] Ariely, Dan. Predictably Irrational, Revised and Expanded Edition: The Hidden Forces That Shape Our Decisions. Harper Perennial, 2010.

to the measured objectivity of the early majority, and with most of the organization ready to proceed, the resistance increases again. It is important at this stage to remember that it is not a personal attack or an ignorant revolt against progress, but the consequence of an honestly held perspective. Moreover, they are brave enough to go against the majority who support an initiative. Their feedback and concerns should be addressed with due consideration and positive attribution. Beyond basic respect, it ensures a productive long-term relationship that is not marred by a dismissive end run.

What to do:

• Break up the journey. Providing a comprehensive view of an initiative all the way to sustainment can give earlier cohorts a sense of completeness but make this group weary when the effort and potential points of failure are displayed together. Frame the journey in phases and provide assurances of support at each step.

• Point to early majority adopters. While early majority were looking for the objectivity provided by their more progressive peers, the late majority is looking for simple numbers. Pointing to other parts of the organization who are adopting a new process or technology, who this group sees as being sensible, provides this group a defensible position from which to make their hesitant entry.

What not to do:

• Over-invest. This group will never advocate for change, and no amount of effort will convert them into evangelists. Direct your effort towards previous cohorts who will, in turn, keep this recalcitrant group aligned with the project.

• Compromise. Being naturally hesitant to change, this

group will often try to reduce their anxiety by negotiating terms that minimize the impact to them. While using skeuomorphs to reduce perceived change is beneficial, compromising on the integrity or functionality of an initiative to gain their approval is counterproductive. Adoption by this group should be considered an outcome of good planning and change management, not a core consideration.

## Laggard

At the far end of the continuum are those who actively oppose new processes and technology. There will always be a group who morally oppose technical advancement. In a 1985 paper by Barbara Baran, she writes, "[…] resistance to automation within the user community proved to be an equally serious barrier to diffusion of the new technologies. Professionals, managers, and even executive secretaries balked at the introduction of machinery that threatened to transform the character of their work and the relations of power in their workplaces. In the past few years, it has taken a dramatic change in the competitive dynamics of the industry to begin to erode this resistance."[133]

In The Ballad of John Henry, a popular 1800s folk song, a railroad driver is pitted against a competing steam engine to prove the technology. John dies of exhaustion in the end, but not before singing, "a man is nothing but a man, but before I let your steam drill beat me down, I'd die with a hammer in my hand." It is frightening to lose relevance, and many would give anything to maintain the status quo.

---

[133] Hegewisch, Ariane, Chandra Childers, and Heidi Hartmann. Women, Automation, and the Future of Work. 2019.

The proportion of laggards in organizations has declined with the increasing proportion of millennials and Gen Z who have grown up around technology. Despite this, there are many naturalists and melancholy people who romanticize pre-agrarian civilization and see their opposition to automation as an important part of their personality. Though a logical skeptic can be dislodged from their position with evidence and the visible support of their peers, for those who oppose initiatives on ethical grounds, there is little that can be done. Discussions about adoption will quickly devolve into vague philosophical discourse. Countless change initiatives have been scuttled by well-intentioned leaders seeking to convince detractors of their error at the expense of building support with more amenable groups.

Change leaders may find themselves spending a lot of time and energy reacting to accusations and refuting claims by these laggards. Acting under the assumption that the detractor does not understand the problem, the leader provides a well-articulated point-by-point defense of the project. It's critical before investing time in this faux debate that the leader realize that the goal of the assailant is not to understand the problem, it is to kill the project. Geeks cannot reason with a detractor whose goal is to stop an initiative by explaining the benefits. Unless there is an openness on the part of the stakeholder, as with the late majority, reactions validate their position and serve only as a time sink.

As always, it is important to acknowledge that for the laggard, they genuinely believe they are doing a good thing by trying to cancel a project. We can maintain positive attribution around their intentions, but we cannot ignore reality. Investing time to convince them will almost always be wasted effort. It is only when they are surrounded by users and advocates that they will submit, turning their attention on some new offense. The best path forward is to sincerely acknowledge their discomfort and redirect them to their peers to de-personalize the situation. The geeks are seen as purveyors of techno-perversions and friendly attempts to reconcile will just provide opportunities for new assaults.

While laggards and vocal detractors can be a challenge in any technical change initiative, the best approach is often the simplest. Avoid, de-escalate, and focus the time of the team with stakeholders who are change-positive.

What to do:

• Acknowledge their discomfort. Regardless of whether their reservations are an emotional response or not, for that person it is real. Refusing to acknowledge them can provoke a more combative response where the target of their misfortune moves from the initiative to its initiator.

• Connect them with peers. As the person or group responsible for their discomfort, they will put little faith in any reassurances you can offer. It is better to create a buddy system where more obliging peers can help them through the process.

What not to do:

• Invest. The best that can be hoped for with laggards is that they will adjust quietly to a new approach; they will never become advocates. Regardless of the improvements seen through a project, they will fondly reflect on the old way of doing things and share a romanticized view with others. Let the natural momentum of change be the catalyst, and do not actively plan for their adoption.

• React. Their objections to an initiative will rarely be on its technical or operational merit, but as a moral battle against larger societal forces. No amount of research or conversations will shift their deeply held views. Deviating from the narrative or making concessions to them will only raise questions from other stakeholders.

## Business Functions

Generational differences and technical posture offer reliable ways to categorize stakeholders, but it requires time and research to understand where to classify them. During the first encounter, we are aware, typically, of only their business function. Though not as consistent as other categories and often weak as an indicator of technical disposition, it is a good starting point to develop the picture of a person.

Each business function has standard motivations and concerns, based on their history of interactions with the technology practice. The sophistication of the organization or the individual's vintage often has a more pronounced impact. However, when considered alongside other factors, the professional domain becomes a valuable tool to inform a communication plan, helping geeks gain a better understand of their stakeholders.

## Accounting & Finance

Though less likely to be involved in initiatives outside of their own domain, people in financial functions have such specific idiosyncrasies that they warrant specific consideration.

Those in financial roles know the business well and are personally well integrated with leadership. Being so attuned with the organization's health, they have a sense for materiality within the different divisions and can advise on what initiatives are worth pursuing. Their intuitive and pragmatic view of value makes them strong allies if they can be convinced of a project's merit.

As clients, they exhibit practicality and optimism. Initiatives supporting their processes, automating elements, or enhancing data quality will garner easy and open support. Due to the criticality and time sensitivity of their work, risk management is crucial. However, demonstrating awareness of their constraints and a willingness to collaborate is often enough to satisfy their inherent risk aversion.

The cyclical and somewhat monastic nature of their work gives them a different sense of time than other functions. Rather than seeing time in terms of months and years, they often frame it around business days. Their planning and their view of projects and initiatives revolve around how they fit within their monthly cycle, and any dependencies need to lie on the prescribed days. In *A Tale of Two* Cities, Mr. Lorry tells Ms. Manette, "I pass my whole life, Miss, on turning an immense pecuniary mangle." Any dependencies, communication, or requests for support, needs to be between turns of that mangle.

The counterpoint to this is that the absolutism inherent in their work makes them very binary. If any component is missing, the project will be deemed a failure. Therefore, it is critical to present plans that are clear and achievable, and a strict division between immediate changes and future features. They will rarely tolerate noncompliant work, holding their partners to the same standards that they hold for themselves.

Once on side they can be a powerful ally. Their pragmatism and authority can lend significant weight to any project that they support.

What to do:

• Be deterministic. Have confidence in your numbers and avoid anything that is approximate. Present ranges rather than probabilities.

• Share an alternate history. This group speaks through corporate artifacts like income statements and balance sheets, and the best way to motivate them is through these reports. Rather than claiming an initiative improves returns by 5 percent, show the income statement for the previous quarter had it been already implemented.

What not to do:

• Be vague. There is nothing in accounting that allows for approximations or analysis that is directionally correct. It is entirely acceptable to make assumptions if those are stated clearly, but uncertainty can erode confidence in the initiative.

• Focus on visualizations. The power that infographics have on demystifying data is lost on financial professionals and is often interpreted as a childish concession. Ignore best practices, and keep the raw information front and center, placing summaries in the appendix.

## Human Resources & Communications

Along a continuum of all possible career paths, few roles would be further apart than those of geeks and HR professionals. The orientation towards order and tractability that draws people into technical fields are the same characteristics that would make them ill-suited for the ambiguity inherent in HR and communications roles. The motivations and priorities can be so different as to seem alien. Fortunately, these differences can make them incredible partners to the technology function. Building strong relationships with people in these roles can be mutually beneficial, as they often complement each other, filling professional gaps.

In building that relationship, it is crucial to understand the likely perspective that people in these roles have towards technology. Often, a fascination with people leads to a career in these areas. Unless they have had personal exposure to technology practitioners, they may see them as a dehumanizing force. There may be a fear that the drive towards conformity that technology represents can lead to white-collar workers losing control, changing their roles from that of skilled specialists to data entry, focused on feeding decision support systems.[134] Without articulating the vision for technology as being in support of people, it can be perceived as a reduction in autonomy, both of their staff and themselves.

When seeking to build relationships with these human-centric roles, we must avoid confirming their suspicions that geeks see nature and people as inputs for technical operations. We cannot outright reject technology; it is crucial to understand and articulate its risks to mitigate them. To establish trust, it's essential to frame technology as a means of revealing human realities, not of creating distance between us.

HR and communications should certainly be involved in projects that effect their own systems or have organizational impacts. However, cultivating strong relationships with these groups can be helpful for all projects. Understanding the behaviors and culture of an organization can facilitate greater

---

[134] Graeber, David. The Utopia of Rules: On Technology, Stupidity, and the Secret Joys of Bureaucracy. Melville House, 2016.

adoption and assist practitioners in framing their work appropriately.

What to do:

• Speak in human terms. While it's worth mentioning the business rationale for a particular opportunity, they do not need to be sold on the commercial merits as much as understanding the human impact. Rather than focusing on the changes in business metrics, describe the change in daily activities or resourcing requirements.

• Consider industry and regional trends. Competitor actions, technical alternatives, and thought leadership, which can be irrelevant distractions for many stakeholders, give this group valuable context and build trust.

What not to do:

• Oversimplify. These are sophisticated business functions led by people who have been at the forefront of every major event for the organization. Respect their experience and intelligence by providing a comprehensive analysis.

• Hide the impact. Certain projects will lead to terminations and be poorly received. Attempting to present a project in an overly positive light to gain their support can hinder their ability to assist you in crafting mitigation plan.


## Sales & Marketing

Few people are as relentless and resilient as those in sales and marketing. The demanding nature of their work, marked by continuous pressure and sales targets, filters out anyone without a hardy constitution. For a savvy geek, this means that if a project is proposed that has a positive impact on a sales-person's metrics, there will be no fiercer advocate.

One risk is that, due to a hyperfocus on specific metrics, they may encourage other important elements to be discarded to be quicker to market. People with more compliant person-alities can be quickly railroaded by a charismatic salesperson promising a superior end product, only to later find themselves abandoned. It is important to not take this personally and re-alize that they are incented to action. Their personality drives them to execute, often struggling to grasp the broader and longer-term implications of a project.

This group is the most vocal advocate for the customer but does so through a self-interested lens of increasing revenue. Balancing their perspective with those of people from strategy, operations, or communications is essential. Establishing rela-tionships early on, highlighting the mutual benefits of such an arrangement, can also aid in gaining buy-in from other stake-holders.

These people excel at breaking down personal barriers and have a natural ability to find the right angle. Leveraging these relationships judiciously for support with difficult stakeholders can be beneficial, provided the geek is prepared to repay their debts.

What to do:

• Focus on outcome. This group is continuously as-sessed on specific metrics that directly affect their compensa-tion. Anything that can improve those metrics will capture their attention.

• Describe the impact across many horizons. Any suc-cesses this group has are forgotten every quarter as their targets are reset. Understanding how an initiative will impact their work this month, next quarter, and next year, is necessary to gain their support.

What not to do:

• Waver. Getting distracted with technical alternatives, internal change management, or other project elements that don't directly impact revenue will quickly diminish interest.

• Forget the customer. Stakeholders in this group need assurance that a project thoroughly considers customer experience. They will not support initiatives where CX has not been meticulously addressed. Be prepared to discuss in detail how a project will impact the customer at every touchpoint.

## Operations

Civil engineers are notorious for designing structures that cannot be created in the real world. Issues with the sequencing of events, the clearances around assemblies, and the lack of consideration for moving materials only become clear during the construction process, not when an engineer is developing the project. In the construction industry changes to the plan will be made at every step, culminating in final product that can be much different from the original design.

The challenges faced by technology workers mirror those of engineers. What appears as a viable approach in theoretical planning can prove impractical during implementation. Technology workers, afflicted with professional myopia, often see the technology itself as the product. We need to consciously elevate our thinking and recognize that the true value lies in operationalization. We need to begin always with the end in mind and work backwards to ensure that the technical solution aligns seamlessly with practical requirements.

This approach requires a strong relationship with people in operations. Those relationships are difficult to build, and easy to damage, so should be carefully guarded. In many organizations, there exists a mutual distrust; from the operational standpoint, the geek is a naïve techie encroaching on their territory. This view is not entirely fair but is very justifiable. From a geek's perspective, operations obstructs their projects and seems unable to recognize the benefits. Again, this view is not entirely fair, but is justifiable. It's essential to empathize with each other's perspectives, recognizing that individuals in operations are closest to the customer and the workface. They possess the deepest understanding of the business and will ultimately bear the consequences of a poorly planned project.

Theories of management are too neat and clean for the real world and try to make sense of decisions after the fact. When we enforce strict adherence, it blinds us to the real impacts.[135] People in operations are the ultimate pragmatists, adept at quickly identifying areas where a project may fail.

Respect operations, get their input early, and build a project plan that includes guard rails. Involve front line staff as much as possible, and consider them your clients, not your obstacles.

What to do:

• Gather their input early. Every technology project should begin with operationalization in mind. Include them from the start to understand the operational boundaries of a project.

---

[135] Abrahamson, Eric, and David H. Freedman. A Perfect Mess: The Hidden Benefits of Disorder. Back Bay Books, 2008.

- Be open to feedback. Organizations live or die on the strength of their operations, and a technology project that introduces friction for employees or customers will quickly erode credibility in the technology function. Operational concessions, even if they introduce complexity, are necessary.

What not to do:

- Dictate. Front-line employees know best the challenges that they face, and the opportunities for streamlining.

- Ignore edge cases. Prepare to speak to every eventuality when a project is implemented. Understand what happens if a system fails, if somebody forgets a password, or if the internet connection goes down. Operations needs to know how to react in every possible situation.

## Strategy

Working with strategy professionals can seem so far removed from daily activities and initiatives that the immediate value is hard to recognize. When we want to move quickly on a project, they delay us with tedious deliberation. While often frustrating, we need to recall that they have a wider view both across the organization and over time. They see the entire chessboard, and that ability can help place your initiative in a broader context.

They know the competitive landscape, what other organizations are working on, and where their company is benchmarked against industry norms. They influence the direction of the company, and initiatives that do not align with these strategic shifts can be discarded.

If a strong personal relationship exists, they also can guide you on how to frame something to gain executive support. Understanding the goals for each function, and, in some cases, the incentives of each executive, allows them to provide advice on how to gain support and identify suitable champions for larger initiatives.

We need to exercise caution before shoehorning technology initiatives into a larger strategic plan. There is evidence against the benefits of strict strategic planning, as it leaves the corporation blind to options and commits them to a path without the flexibility to be dynamic to changes in the market[136]. Technology is a broad organizational enabler, and we need to be able to shift our approaches in response to these changes. Be savvy about negotiating with this group and highlight the aspects of a project that are unassailable.

Although deciphering their opaque language and mysticism may be challenging, adopting their higher and longer-term perspective can lead to a mutually beneficial relationship.

What to do:

• Align to goals. Articulating how an initiative supports key strategic pillars will help to build support from the strategy function.

• Think broadly. Prepare to discuss the implications of the project from the perspective of hardware, software, operations, the customers, future staffing, etc. Breadth is more important than depth.

What not to do:

• Mimic them. The words they use have meaning, and

---

[136] Starbuck, William H. Organizational Realities: Studies of Strategizing and Organizing. Oxford University Press, 2006.

clumsily mashing buzzwords together to build comradery only diminishes credibility.

• Assume. Often part of the inner circle, stakeholders in strategy may be aware of long-term initiatives that conflict with your own. Lay out all impacts so that they can properly advise on how it fits in with the bigger picture, recognizing that requirements for confidentiality may not allow them to provide direct feedback.

## Contextualization

After categorizing the individual based on their generational cohort, their technical posture, and their business function, adjustments need to be made based on the culture of the organization. Forward-thinking digitally native companies with an entrepreneurial workforce might have different needs and priorities compared to underfunded public sector clients. Industries themselves present unique constraints and considerations; implementing new tools for a retailer is differs greatly from doing so for a federally regulated financial institution. Deploying machine learning for wastewater treatment facilities has far greater risks than doing so for a targeted marketing campaign. All attempts to understand individual technical postures must be seen through this organizational and industry lens.

The previous categories are inherent and indelible; a natural innovator cannot consciously become a laggard, and a baby boomer cannot become Gen X. In contrast, corporate culture is more like a hat that individuals can put on or take off as they transition to new roles. As people work with different organizations and industries, the number of hats they have increases. Researching a person's past roles through social media can provide insights into their professional history and which organizational culture they might favor. Convincing a senior leader in a risk-averse organization, even if they are a natural early adopter, can be challenging as they echo the prevailing culture. In early conversations, encourage them to change their hat by discussing how similar challenges were addressed in their previous roles. Establish a sense of camaraderie and convey your progressive perspective, using this foundation to seek their advice on convincing skeptics.

In the 1960s, Dr. Eric Berne introduced the concept of transactional analysis, which states that individuals have three ego states: parent, adult, and child, each with its own set of beliefs and behaviors. When we interact with our respected peers, we are each adopting an adult ego state, and that understanding, though never explicitly acknowledged, is required for the discussion to be meaningful.[137] However, when feeling overwhelmed, confused, or experiencing imposter syndrome, people shift to a childlike state. In this state, responding to an adult-like approach from a peer might result in a childlike response. A defensive stakeholder who undervalues the technology function may approach conversations from a parental state, potentially harboring subconscious resentment when met with an adult response from an offended geek.

Effective communication relies on recognizing and navigating the ego states of both us and our stakeholders. Awareness of our own state and that of our stakeholders is crucial for meaningful conversations. When we fail to understand our stakeholders, our communication style may inadvertently push

---

[137] Berne, Eric. Games People Play: The Basic Handbook of Transactional Analysis. Ballantine Books, 1996. Originally published in 1964.

them into a social posture that hinders collaboration. Contextualizing communication to the individual, considering their inherent characteristics discussed earlier, empowers us to navigate and adapt to different ego states.

## Challenges

Every person is unique, possessing distinct views on technology, levels of understanding, and personal motivations. It is impossible to predict with certainty how a millennial laggard accountant working in the public sector will respond to a specific approach. While combining generational differences, technical posture, and organizational context provides a useful starting point with categories that can be quickly assumed, a savvy geek must also be cognizant of additional confounding factors and individual challenges that may influence the person's response.

### People are naturally fearful of technology

In a 1997 interview with George Lucas by Kevin Kelly, Lucas is asked if technology is making the world better or worse, and gives the following response:

"If you watch the curve of science and everything we know, it shoots up like a rocket. We're on this rocket and we're going perfectly vertical into the stars. But the emotional intelligence of humankind is equally if not more important than our intellectual intelligence. We're just as emotionally illiterate as we were 5000 years ago; so emotionally our line is completely horizontal. The problem is the horizontal and the vertical are getting farther and farther apart. And as these things grow apart, there's going to be some kind of consequence of that."[138]

If the creator of *Star Wars* has such deep uncertainty on the ultimate impact of technology (perhaps that is why he placed the franchise in the distant past), we cannot expect the average person to have a naturally positive disposition. Even Elon Musk, who believes himself divinely mandated to take humanity to Mars, cautions that artificial intelligence could lead to the destruction of civilization.[139]

We have a natural aversion to change. Even if we manage to overcome our genetic imperative to avoid new things, we confront the deeper question of what comes next. Kafka expressed his anxieties about the future to his girlfriend Felice, who worked as a seller of dictation devices. He was terrified, predicting a future where we would become "degraded factory workers." He believed that machines would one day talk to us, suggest restaurants, and correct our pronunciation.[140] In ancient Greece, Socrates believed that the rise of literacy would lead to forgetfulness and diminish oratory. People thought that the electrification of homes would endanger children, and that women would explode if a train travelled faster than 50 miles an hour.[141] There is a deep-seated fear of technology that has persisted across our history.

Geeks must recognize the discomfort experienced by their stakeholders, understanding that they are seen as a human representation of the societal changes associated with technology.

---

[138] Kelly, Kevin. What Technology Wants. Penguin Books, 2011.
[139] Duffy, Clare, and Ramishah Maruf. "Elon Musk warns AI could cause 'civilization destruction' even as he invests in it." CNN Business, 2023.
[140] Latham, Martin. Booksellers Tale. Penguin Press, 2021.
[141] Rooney, Ben. "Women and Children First: Technology and Moral Panic." Wall Street Journal, July 11, 2011.

Our contributions are modest when looked at independently, but taken in aggregate, each re-platforming, automation, new machine learning framework, and business intelligence report contributes to a more technology-driven workplace. Even if our colleagues like us as people, they worry about what we represent. Understanding and accepting this is important to building an authentic relationship where they are comfortable sharing those concerns.

## People have too many choices

There is great benefit in a partnership where the geek brings technical know-how, and the stakeholder brings domain knowledge. But in our pursuit of this merger of skillsets, we can go too far and drive outside of our respective lanes. We should maintain ownership of the technology aspect and guide stakeholders toward appropriate alternatives, but not own business decisions; our role is to enable.

With the best of intentions, we compile a list of alternatives for stakeholders based on the individual project and all compounding factors. Whether this comes from a diffusion of responsibility or genuine attempt at transparency, it only serves to erode confidence. We should not aspire to a completely technocratic organization, but the more democratic groups are, and the more decisions that people have to make, the worse off they are.[142] The more choices we are given, the less satisfied we are going to be.[143] Technology leaders need to give very few,

---

[142] Achen, Christopher, and Larry Bartels. Democracy for Realists: Why Elections Do Not Produce Responsive Government. Princeton University Press, 2016.
[143] Schwartz, Barry. Paradox of Choice: Why More is Less. Harper Perennial, 2004.

very precise choices, and celebrate the stakeholder when they make steps down the path that we have created for them.

## People lack psychological safety

No matter how much effort we put into change management and human factors, if people do not feel safe, they are not going to voluntarily adopt new technologies. Every new initiative carries risk, and if the potential consequences of failure outweigh the benefits of success, there is no incentive to participate. When people feel generally unsafe at work, that unbalances the scales towards conservatism.

Workplace psychological safety is often promoted through organizational policies that encourage employees to "bring their full selves" to work and emphasize inclusivity. While many corporations make progress on paper and comply with legislation regarding accommodations, the underlying organizational culture often does not fully align with these goals.

During the 2010s, legacy organizations embraced the Silicon Valley mentality of "failing fast", influenced by popular business books like *Fail Fast, Fail Often*. Leaders were encouraged to celebrate failures as valuable learning opportunities. However, this approach sometimes led to a shift in evaluating performance, with leaders counting the number of attempts rather than focusing on successful outcomes.

Over time, the phrase "fail fast" has become a managerial bromide, and employees may hesitate to take significant risks if organizational policies do not support this approach. In recent years, the emphasis has shifted from simply failing to learning from failures. If advocates cannot articulate the underlying benefits of a failed project, it can impact their career prospects.[144]

We need to ensure that there is a tolerance for mistakes in our organizations and take the time to debrief to uncover the resulting learnings. We should also encourage risk taking in our reports, especially by encouraging them to speak up and share their ideas. But we cannot elevate the practice by sharing the number of failures we have had; we should evaluate ourselves solely by the value we create.

This does not preclude an organization from being psychologically safe, it simply reinforces the need for careful planning and a focus on human factors. Technology comes with challenges; we simply need to be transparent on the risks and orient our teams endlessly towards value.

### People lack data literacy

In 2020, a deadly hurricane was approaching Florida. News and weather agencies provided a regularly updated infographic featuring a "zone of certainty" to keep residents informed. The zone incorporated stochastic meteorological models that displayed the likely path of the hurricane, with the boundaries representing the deviation from the best estimate. As the hurricane approached, the model's uncertainty decreased, causing the boundaries to narrow. It was found afterwards that only 18% of residents understood how to interpret the infographic.[145] They mistakenly believed that the constricting boundaries indicated a smaller impact. Lives were endangered

---

144 DePrisco, Michael. "How to transition from a 'fail fast' mentality to a 'learn fast' mindset." Forbes, January 12, 2022.
145 ThoughtSpot, "9 data and analytics trends for 2023", 2022.

due to a lack of statistical understanding. But we cannot reasonably expect the general public to have this level of understanding; the fault was not theirs but with the meteorologists for their lack of empathy.

The lack of data literacy makes people unable to describe their problem-space. They can point to symptoms and describe past events, but they cannot articulate systemic issues. When we ask them what they want, they struggle to think of anything but the solution-space.[146] This underscores the importance of collaboration. We need to use these gaps to define the problem-space through contextual inquiry and customer discovery. Understanding our stakeholders needs to be the first step.

Most people are simply not equipped to understand data. There is a reason that pie charts still exist. Overcomplicating analyses or providing excessive detail does not fortify our case; rather, it obscures it. We need to understand the level of technical understanding before crafting our messaging.

### Embedding Empathy

Leaders and often have strong relationships with their peers in the organization formed over time and shared experiences. However, individual contributors often hide their humanity when adopting their professional personas. They use formal language, adopt patrician airs, and show their professionalism by being aloof.

This disconnect is not only damaging to the practice but also fosters an atmosphere of tension within the team. Being

---

[146] Olsen, Dan. Lean Product Playbook: How to Innovate with Minimum Viable Products and Rapid Customer Feedback. Wiley, 2015.

implicitly or explicitly compelled to suppress social instincts to follow checklists and processes designed for technical convenience prevents people from being integrated wholes. Geeks are put into a position of having to ignore process to align with stakeholders; otherwise, they must willingly frustrate them for bureaucratic compliance. While leaders often verbally encourage empathy, the lack of autonomy and demands for submission send conflicting messages.

Technology workers are at their best when they have the freedom to be creative within certain boundaries, and to adapt their approach based on the relationships and organizational understandings they have. Within their teams, they need to be free to enjoy an eclecticism without shame, and to be authentic with their colleagues. As Kierkegaard wrote, "the most common form of despair is not being who you are."

When we are self-absorbed, seeing only what is directly in front of us, we kill empathy. In *Social Intelligence*, Dan Goleman writes, "Our world contracts as our problems and preoccupations loom large. But when we focus on others, our world expands."[147] Maintaining a service mindset is non-negotiable, but we must also allow people the space for emotional expression. We should meet the professional standards of our stakeholders, leaving the hoodies at home, but let us be safely weird. Empathy cannot be coerced; it must rise naturally.

This is not just a platitude – there is a significant commercial upside. Employees who report having positive social interactions in the workplace have higher job satisfaction[148] and lower

---

[147] Goleman, Daniel. Social Intelligence: The New Science of Human Relationships. Bantam Books, 2006.
[148] Nolan, T. & Küpers, W. (2009). Organizational climate, organizational culture, and workplace relationships. In R. L. Morrison & S. L. Wright (Eds.), Friends and enemies in organizations (pp. 57–

turnover.[149] These positive interactions echo throughout the organization and lead to greater shared experiences and the development of more trusting relationships.[150]

As this trust develops, team members engage in more positive, cooperative behavior. This, in turn, leads to more proactive and altruistic behaviors such as team members independently guiding and advising their colleagues.[151]

People are by their nature creative, active, productive beings. To bring out their best, work must be attractive and engaging.[152] It is time to stop increasingly standardizing each task and embrace a shift away from Taylorism. By affording our teams creative liberties, we empower them and instill a sense of ownership in their work.

The personal benefits of empathy are evident, but they can only be fully realized when individuals are free to practice it. Leaders play a critical role by embedding empathy into team processes, inspiring its cultivation among their reports, and encouraging stakeholders to expect it of the function.

---

77). Palgrave Macmillan.
[149] Moynihan, D. P., & Pandey, S. K. (2008). The Ties That Bind: Social Networks, Person-Organization Value Fit, and Turnover Intentions. Journal of Public Administration Research and Theory, 18, 205-227.
[150] Oh, Hongseok, Myung-Ho Chung, and Giuseppe Labianca. "Group Social Capital and Group Effectiveness: The Role of Informal Socializing Ties." The Academy of Management Journal 47, no. 6 (2004): 860–75.
[151] Hamilton, E. A. (2007). Firm friends: Examining functions and outcomes of workplace friendship among law firm associates. Dissertation Abstracts International Section A: Humanities and Social Sciences, 68(3-A), 1068.
[152] Herzberg, F.I. Work and the nature of man. World, 1966.

## Five Tips for Leveraging Empathy

### 1. Walk the talk

Leaders cannot merely encourage empathy and intentional relationship-building in their reports; they must personally exemplify these behaviors. Achieving this in an authentic way can be challenging, as without authenticity, efforts appear awkward and contradictory.

As a leader, openly sharing your struggles, experiences, and decision-making process is one of the simplest ways to demonstrate empathy. During standup meetings, go beyond technical challenges and delve into the social obstacles and stakeholder dynamics. Discuss the impact of politics on decisions and share the history behind process changes, highlighting key players involved. Importantly, focus on understanding the motivations of detractors rather than attacking them personally. It can be great to inject good-natured humor, but swiftly redirect the conversation toward identifying root causes and collaboratively determining an approach to address them.

Change can be challenging when an outsider mindset is entrenched within the team. However, people are adaptable and can shift their dominant personas based on the situation, given enough time and pressure. A study by researcher Richard Savin-Williams observed boys at a summer camp who consistently organized themselves into familiar hierarchies: a leader, a joker, a geek, a bully, and so on. When Savin-Williams reformed them into homogeneous groups of all leaders or all bullies, initial conflict and positioning for dominance occurred. Eventually, they fell into the familiar pattern, adopting the personalities of alternative archetypes.[153] We all have dormant

---

[153] Freedman, Daniel G. Human Sociobiology: A Holistic Approach. Free Press, 1979.

leader, bully, geek, and joker personalities within us. It's a matter of consciously bringing out the persona that suits the situation.

People are also driven to mimic the behavior of those they see as holding a higher position than them. What leaders demonstrate in front of their reports, their teams are more likely to adopt. Prosocial behaviors come about when people see others exhibiting those behaviors.[154]

The complication is that we cannot simply mandate a particular culture. Culture arises naturally from the conventions of the team. Leaders need to make personal changes to show these conventions.

One example of this is in the lexicon of the team. All practitioners look to their leader to set the tone for how the team operates. If the leader divides the organization into "us" and "them", uses negative language, assumes malice in stakeholders, and disparages vendors, those behaviors will manifest in the team. There is some cohesive value in a team that feels it is in a battle, but that battle needs to be against inefficient processes, not against other people.

Changes in language can extend to how we encourage each other. Focusing on the character of our team members rather than just their behavior helps internalize empathetic characteristics. For example, say "you are a very considerate person" rather than, "that was nice of you." Avoid and discourage dismissive phrases such as "I would have", as well as self-promotion by favoring "I" rather than "we."[155] Leaders should very

---

154 Eisenberg, N., and Mussen, P. H. The roots of prosocial behavior in children. Cambridge University Press, 1989.
155 Borba, Michele. UnSelfie: Why Empathetic Kids Succeed in Our All-About-Me World. Touchstone, 2017.

visibly put away their phone to encourage team mates to do the same, as the sight of phones during a conversation is shown to reduces empathy and understanding.[156] Every subtle shift in team norms has an impact.

Establishing empathy in a team cannot be treated as a checklist, it needs to be a totality of action. It involves both legalistic aspects, where formal policies mandate specific behaviors, and conventional elements. Executive decrees can set rules, but the social reinforcement from peers is essential for effective implementation. These customs and policies work redundantly yet synergistically to guide the team.

In the heat of the moment, everybody gets irritated and seeks an outlet. We have all been frustrated by stakeholders who surprise us at the last moment with new requirements. Genuinely sharing that frustration with the team is fine, and in itself being empathetic with them, but what happens next is critical. If leaders leave it there, and angrily adjust the project to meet that new requirement, it fosters an environment where stakeholders are seen as nuisances hindering our work. On the other hand, if, after a therapeutic moment, leaders walk their team through their thought process, identify the source of the misunderstanding, ideate on ways to prevent such issues, and take an optimistic view that considers stakeholder feedback as valuable, it materializes an environment where stakeholders are seen as partners. They may be occasionally frustrating, but ultimately, their feedback enhances our work.

Leaders cannot present empathy as a step on a checklist but

---

156 Przybylski, A. K., & Weinstein, N. (2013). Can you connect with me now? How the presence of mobile communication technology influences face-to-face conversation quality. Journal of Social and Personal Relationships, 30(3), 237–246.

must showcase it daily to establish it in their team. It is only by walking the talk that we can build it as a core capability.

## 2. Observe before acting

Most experienced technology workers have learned the hard way the importance of understanding a situation before proposing solutions. As we progress from implementors to leaders, we instinctively revert to our roots and run headlong into the technical aspects of problems, realizing too late that we're surrounded by landmines. No matter how many times we have been burned, it can be difficult to restrain ourselves, and we can often find that we are thinking through potential alternatives before our stakeholders have even finished describing their situation.

Before we begin to reorient our teams, we need to exhaustively survey and understand the current state and to understand the complex interrelationships that exist. This involves delving into the intricate interrelationships that exist within the team and placing them within a broader organizational context. A nuanced understanding of these dynamics is essential before attempting to enhance the position or address the concerns of individual stakeholders. The interconnected nature of these relationships demands a careful examination of potential butterfly effects, ensuring that actions taken to benefit one stakeholder do not inadvertently negatively affect others. This foresight is crucial for effective leadership and strategic decision-making.

We systematically evaluate technical changes by placing a new tool in an isolated sandbox, integrating it into our existing toolset, checking for security vulnerabilities, consulting our network for insights, and thoroughly understanding its potential impact before adopting and deploying it to production. This same systematic approach should be applied to how we work with people.

Every individual operates within a complex network, both inside and outside the organization. Past experiences within their function and industry shape their frame of reference. No amount of categorization based on generational cohorts or business functions can fully capture what drives a person's behavior.

It is crucial to allow individuals the time needed for their character to emerge. Presuppositions should not be the sole basis for assessment, and initial reactions to a situation should not be the sole evidence for permanently labeling someone as a friend or foe. We must remain fluid in our assessments, letting new information change our perspectives. Over time, champions may become dejected, and those who were ambivalent may become newly inspired toward technological change.

Observe before acting to make sure that you have the measure of your stakeholders.

### 3. Make it part of performance management

In most disciplines, geeks adhere to a routinized cycle of sprints and user stories. They work apart from their managers and leads, who interact with stakeholders and product managers, making them doubly removed from the end customer. While forward-thinking relationship-focused leaders can say all the right things, without incentivization, it will always appear as an extra-credit activity rather than a core expectation for the practitioner.

If we evaluate our employees based solely on their technical performance, we cannot expect them to prioritize individuals over technology. We need to continuously monitor and measure our social and personal impact. When our actions do not align with our words, and we promote and reward churlish technical mercenaries over integrative peacemakers, our teams notice it, and they will behave accordingly.

The challenge of establishing subjective performance metrics based on how they made stakeholders feel is aggravated by the comparative ease of evaluating sprint velocity. Pushing through that difficulty, in open communication with the rest of the team, is worthwhile and should be part of a larger conversation on what a productive, healthy technology function looks like. Often, we assign arbitrary numbers to a process, create a complex system of counterincentives, and feel satisfied that we have created order from chaos, but this is illusory.

Management by solely quantitative metrics will always lead to gaming. When leaders evaluate their reports based on story points, it incentivizes developers to sandbag their estimates to move up the leaderboard. When we respond by creating a peer review estimating process, we create a barter system where developers team up against their scrum masters. If we want to maximize our impact, we need to realize that we must find out how well we have supported people. We should not be satisfied with clumsy proxies.

We need to ensure that practitioners have an opportunity to interact with the end customer. Genuine, non-productive social contact between people with mutual distrust will breed familiarity; over time, this will lead to friendship.

In Maine, at a camp called Seeds of Peace International, kids from warring nations are put together. Regardless of their initial feelings toward each other, by the end of their time together, friendships naturally arise. When interviewed, the participants reported feeling more positive about each other and were more trusting, even years later.[157] The more exposure we have to each other, the more we come to care about each other. It is easy to dismiss a request from an anonymous coworker, but when we know the person behind the ask, we naturally respond with empathy.

Collaborate with the Human Resources department to develop a performance management framework that rewards the correct behaviors, is defensible, and aligns with organizational objectives. Through formalized debrief sessions with stakeholders, gather documentation on non-technical developmental opportunities for team members, and provide continuous aggregated and anonymized feedback to the individual and the team. Rather than acting as a relay, delivering criticisms to the team in a ritualized retrospective, be a lens that focuses and summarizes the feedback, facilitating discussions on how to respond to their comments.

When offering feedback to the team, ensure that it is personalized and meaningful. Simply acknowledging stakeholder feedback is insufficient; delve deeper to pinpoint specific individuals and incidents, both positive and negative. Humans inherently seek recognition of their value from others, but it's a relative measure rather than an absolute one. If everyone receives the same acclaim, it becomes valueless. Recognition is a zero-sum game. Seek opportunities to celebrate individuals who have made a significant impact.

---

[157] Schroeder, Juliana, and Jane Risen. "Peace through friendship." New York Times, August 24, 2014.

Finally, share these learnings in a respectful way with the entire team. When technical performance is lacking, shaming that individual in front of the team is cruel and unnecessary, but when a particular stakeholder had candid feedback regarding communication abilities, that's a valuable personal insight for the team to know. Non-technical feedback reflects less on the individual than on the conventions of the team.

Performance metrics are designed to encourage positive behaviors in staff and provide management with a means of assessing ability. Empathetic behaviors need to be quantified, assessed, and clearly integrated into variable compensation, career development, and performance discussions. What gets measured gets done, and without incentivizing empathy, we will not see long-term results.

## 4. Embed it in your operating model

Operating models describe how resources are transformed into value. Ideally, the definition of value is derived from the mission statement of the function and the nature of the organization. For an analytics team, this might involve leveraging data to provide insights to decision-makers to improve profitability. For a development team, it could mean building products to enhance user experience. In the case of a systems administrator, the focus might be on managing an environment to reduce risk. These oversimplified input/output models, even in their expanded form, neglect the personal aspects, prioritizing execution over experience. While a strong relationship leading to greater adoption may be viewed as a positive externality, it is rarely treated as a guiding principle.

Best-in-class organizations that are effectively leveraging

their technology practice don't treat relationships as an after-thought; instead, it is integrated into all parts of their operating model. The tools they use, hiring practices, training, and onboarding, are all designed with consideration for usability and experience. The function's output extends beyond the mere delivery of a report, aiming to enhance data literacy and technical evangelization. The mission statement, rather than being a directive to comply, is focused on the holistic creation of value.

Empathy should be ingrained in all phases of the project delivery model. Change management must be a consideration from the earliest stages of ideation. Early socialization of ideas is critical. Discussing them with all involved in advance makes them more palatable when finally revealed. Similar to how people enjoy familiar songs, the familiarity that early discussions can create supports future uptake. Understanding our customers reduces anxiety around new approaches.

The planning component of project delivery presents another opportunity to prioritize the end user. We need to begin with the end in mind and work backward through iterative requirements to arrive at a viable path forward. In a 1997 developer conference interview with Steve Jobs, he famously said, "You need to start with the customer experience and work backward to the technology. You can't start with the technology and try to figure out where you're going to try to sell it."[158] We should never act like a hammer searching for a nail but rather as problem solvers for the people we serve.

As leaders, when we conceptualize and build a healthy and empathetic technology function, we need to start with the end

---

[158] Comments provided during a 1997 WWDC conference in response to a challenge about his technical capabilities.

goal the ultimate output. This output should transcend the simple execution of others' designs. We need to have a hand in shaping these designs to realize the value of the relationship. Acting solely as executors limits the potential for more engaging work and denies our organizations the opportunity for a better-informed product. Each facet of the technology operating model should consider two equally important factors – the technical and the human.

Post-delivery support should likewise be focused on the stakeholder, and not a cold enumeration of mutual responsibilities. The last interaction will be remembered most vividly, and we should make every effort to ensure it is a positive experience.

That stakeholder experience should permeate our work. When we are providing project updates, we need to be speaking in the language of the business. Rather than explicit technical definitions, we should find more digestible ways to describe our progress. Human minds work best with metaphors[159] despite knowing that it is an oversimplification. We are motivated by a complex and often subconscious worldview shaped by our culture and lived experience. We cannot inspire confidence by sharing specifics; we need to shift that onto their mental mapping of the initiative. Even if our stakeholders realize they are flawed approximations, the consistent use of nontechnical metaphors helps them feel more in control.

Despite our best efforts, projects will sometimes fail. Scope may change, and features that were important to a stakeholder may become backlogged. Software may not live up to the promises made by vendors. In the end, stakeholders will not

---

[159] Jaynes, Julian. The Origin of Consciousness in the Breakdown of the Bicameral Mind. Boston: Houghton Mifflin Co., 1976.

only remember what you did, but how you made them feel through the process. Over time, people forget difficulties and their mind constructs a memory that smooths over the rough edges. If you leave people with a positive feeling, they will forget the challenges throughout the project.[160]

When building a new team, we need to create operating models that prioritize people over technology.

## 5. Get comfortable being uncomfortable

There is nothing more psychologically soothing than simply executing somebody else's instructions. Receiving a list of activities for a two-week sprint cycle, orchestrated externally, without the danger of change or personal responsibility, is the ultimate safety net. If an activity is not completed when expected, we can say that it was underestimated. If an approach does not work, we can point to the person who instructed us. As long as a person does what they are told, they have the ability to completely extricate themselves if anything goes wrong.

For most organizations, this toxic view of psychological safety is the implicit goal. Processes and structures are designed to divorce technology workers as much as possible from decision-making. Once they are onboarded, they are largely interchangeable. For our part, we comply, enticed by the opportunity to surrender the more stressful parts of our profession.

For a high-performing practice, and for high-performing in-

---

[160] Loftus, Elizabeth. Memory, Surprising new insights into how we remember and why we forget. Reading, Mass: Addison-Wesley Publishing Co., 1980.

dividuals, it is essential that we have a different type of psychological safety. We need to create environments where safety does not come through the transfer of risk, but where we can encounter risk in a supportive way. To have a psychologically safe team it is critical to give them the ability to speak their minds. According to Amy Edmonson, "psychological safety in the workplace is the belief that the environment is safe for interpersonal risk-taking. It is a belief that one will not be punished or humiliated for speaking up with ideas, questions, concerns, or mistakes."[161] Safety needs to be about the ability to take risks, not the ability to avoid stress.

We also need to be the peacemakers, willing be the first ones to take steps towards to redefining our relationships. In the 1980s, computer scientist Robert Axelrod created a tournament of computer simulations to determine the winning long-term strategy for the prisoner's dilemma game. He found that the best solution was "tit for tat"; cooperation with those who cooperated in the past, and not cooperating with those who haven't previously. Over time, even if it begins as self-interest, we move towards community and collaboration.[162] When we wallow in the past, nothing will improve. One side needs to be the first to try and reframe the relationship. It will take time to overcome past negative experiences, but with consistency, it is possible to have a healthier partnership.

When organizations adopt technology to enhance a legacy process, it aligns with and supports the existing framework. Given the risk involved with integrating technology, business

---

[161] Edmonson, Amy. The Fearless Organization: Creating Psychological Safety in the Workplace for Learning, Innovation, and Growth. Wiley, 2018.
[162] Axelrod, Robert. The Evolution of Cooperation. Basic Books, 1984.

leaders might express a need for explicit details about the approach and the final product, seeking to control all factors of the project. Without open communication, psychological safety, and mutual respect, the resulting product will be inferior and fail to leverage the strengths of either team. We will forever be stuck in tepid incrementalism.

Factories were originally designed around water wheels, transmitting power through a central shaft. When electricity was introduced, rather than directly powering devices, it was initially used to power the vestigial shaft. While this enhanced productivity and reduced uncertainty, it was an incremental improvement. The true value became apparent only when factories were redesigned around electricity. In the same way, when we use technology to energize outdated approaches, we may observe only marginal improvements, making it crucial to be willing to insert our perspectives.

Henry Ford captured this perfectly saying, "If I had asked what they wanted, they would have said a faster horse."[163] To be at our best, we need a challenger mindset and a team of supportive leaders. We need to be comfortable being uncomfortable and insert ourselves into the decision-making process.

### Summary

Even though detractors abound, few are intentionally subversive. People will always act in a way that they genuinely think is best, even if it appears adversarial to others. At the dinner table of a senior marketing executive, mistaking their waning influence for normal industry cycles, they may curse a

---

[163] Apocryphal quote attributed to Ford in the early 2000s.

generative AI project and those involved, seeing it as an expensive fad. From their viewpoint, they are the protagonist trying to protect the organization from missteps, and the leaders of the technology function are cast as villains. Their genuine concern can seem spiteful from our perspective, and we come to see them as enemies. Our retaliations can confirm their suspicions and lead to a passive-aggressive tit-for-tat that jeopardizes the project and, potentially, two careers. We need to always to practice positive attribution and encourage it in our teams to avoid these outcomes.

Stakeholders can become detractors for many reasons. People can easily become entangled in competing commitments, where their unspoken goals conflicts with their stated objectives[164] as they struggle to reduce cognitive dissonance. A common example of this is underperforming people who harbor the belief that if they genuinely applied themselves, they would excel in their work. The danger is that if they did apply themselves and did not excel, they would be forced to confront their personal limitations in a way which that they are likely not prepared. When people reach the limits of their capabilities, they need to explain to themselves and to others why they can progress no further.

Geeks are not immune to this. If a developer has heavily invested in a particular technology stack that has lost relevance, they face one of two choices: either re-invest in a new technology stack and start over, or double down and integrate that technology into their identity. People will almost always choose the path of least resistance to avoid cognitive dissonance. When a leader, tasked with building support for a technology transformation, tries to appeal to an executive, pushing them

---

[164] Kegan, Robert, and Lisa Lahey. "The Real Reason People Won't Change." Harvard Business Review, November 2001.

into a position where they must either acknowledge their declining relevance or declare the technology leader a heretic, the decision is easy.

Successful change management comes down to four essential things: duration, integrity, commitment, and effort.[165] Change needs to be implemented quickly, minimizing uncomfortable transitional periods. The change agents need to have integrity and have built trust in stakeholders. Executive sponsorship and commitment must be clearly exhibited. Finally, it requires collective effort. Most change management frameworks cover these in different ways. Stories are told, buy-in gathered, early adopters identified, their participation is celebrated, executives publicly support the project. However very few of these broadly used frameworks address the need for integrity within the team. Breaking down the barriers to change is a daunting and very human exercise, and we need empathetic individuals to undertake it—especially when technology is involved. In the absence of a dire threat, employees will keep doing what they've always done. We should not simply ask an executive to make a decree but to reach the hearts and minds of the users.

In *What Technology Wants*, Kevin Kelly writes:

"Newness is such an elemental part of our lives today that we forget how rare it was in ancient days. Most change in the past was cyclical: A forest was cleared for a field and then a farm was abandoned; an army came and then an army left. Droughts followed floods, and one king, either good or evil, succeeded another. For most humans, for most of time, real

---

[165] Sirkin, Harold L., Perry Keenan, and Alan Jackson. "The Hard Side of Change Management." Harvard Business Review, October 2005.

change was rarely experienced. What little change did happen occurred over centuries.

And when change erupted it was to be avoided. If historical change had any perceived direction at all, it was downhill. [...] In ancient times when a bearded prophet forecast what was to come, the news was generally bad. The idea that the future brought improvement was never very popular until recently. Even now, progress is far from universally accepted. Cultural advancements are commonly seen as exceptional episodes that may at any moment retreat into the woes of the past."[166]

The difference now is that bearded prophets can have their dreams quashed by stakeholders if they cannot frame the situation appropriately, destroying value for the organization. Empathy is not just touchy-feely; it affects the bottom line and impacts all areas of corporate life. Research indicates that empathy has a positive effect on the health, wellness, resilience, and happiness of workers.[167] It also improves trust, moral courage,[168] and supports inclusivity initiatives.[169] It is essential for success as a leader in any function but is a key differentiator within the technology practice.

When geeks advocate for new processes, they usually do so from a "maximax" perspective, selecting the alternative with

---

[166] Kelly, Kevin. What Technology Wants. Penguin Books, 2011.
[167] Block-Lerner J, Adair C, Plumb JC, Rhatigan DL, Orsillo SM. The case for mindfulness-based approaches in the cultivation of empathy: does nonjudgmental, present-moment awareness increase capacity for perspective-taking and empathic concern? Journal of Marital Family Therapy. 2007 Oct;33(4):501-16.
[168] Gordon, Mary. Roots of Empathy: Changing the World, Child by Child. Thomas Allen Publishers, 2012.
[169] Allport, Gordon. The Nature of Prejudice. Addison-Wesley, 1954.

the highest potential payoff. Conversely, our stakeholders, particularly non-technical leadership, evaluate our proposals using a "maximin" strategy, choosing the alternative with the smallest potential loss. We sell our ideas to ourselves rather than reframing them value according to the decision-making criteria of the decision-makers.

People are far more fearful of losing something than they are pleased by gaining the same amount. They seek certainty in wins but will take significant risks to avoid losses.[170] When geeks propose a new approach, stakeholders perceive the risk of failure as far more significant than the potential gains. Leveraging empathy is about building processes within the practice that appeal to the individual decision makers, rather than to the geeks themselves.

We think of capitalist management as omniscient. Like an economist assuming rationality, the role of management is distilled into a caricature of itself, a caste of rational all-knowing administrators. Those in technical or analytical fields assume that a properly articulated business plan with a clear return will be approved, and we can work in happy isolation. We begin our careers with a glossy view of corporate life. As we grow in tenure and cynicism, we realize that stakeholders are governed as much by personal ambition as anything else.[171] Without that understanding, and the required changes to our approaches, we will never realize our maximum potential.

---

[170] Kahneman, D., & Tversky, A. (1990). Prospect theory: An analysis of decision under risk. In P. K. Moser (Ed.), Rationality in action: Contemporary approaches (pp. 140–170). Cambridge University Press. (Reprinted from "Econometrica" 47 (1979), 263-91.
[171] Braverman, H. Labor and Monopoly Capital: The Degradation of Work in the Twentieth Century. NYU Press, 1998.

# CONCLUSION

*"We have a dozen tables seated we don't have time for this."*

*"We provide an experience, not purple lettuce!"*

One of the best leaders I had the good fortune to work under was a cantankerous Swiss chef who would never allow me to compromise. Whether it was the consistency of my tomatoes diced hours ahead of service, or the accuracy of my plating when we had a full house, he maintained the same exacting standards. Between offensive questions about my parentage and occasional minor abuse, he shared profound insights. I have a strongly held belief that there is no better crucible for personal growth than a restaurant, a belief rooted in the experiences I had under his leadership.

On an especially educational evening, utterly exhausted, I plated a side salad during the dinner rush. The base of the salad was mixed greens but had a conspicuous absence of purple radicchio. Chef, who I had worked alongside until the early hours of that morning and who spent the prior twelve hours in the kitchen with me preparing for dinner, reprimanded me for my poor attention to detail. Absolutely frustrated and exhausted after an eighty-hour week, I argued that it was inconsequential. We were behind, short-staffed, and both operating on almost no sleep. Purple radicchio was not a priority for anyone at that moment.

His reaction was frustrating at the time, but it remains something I reflect on decades later, now in a completely different field. The customer does not know about our situation; they do not care that we are exhausted. We had served dozens of tables that evening, but for the customer, it was a singular experience. This might have been a wedding anniversary. It may have been their first date. They may be celebrating a personal achievement. If we yield an inch because we are tired, we are doing so at their expense.

*"That's been under the heat lamp for 5 minutes, put it back in the oven."*

*"I can't, we need to get this table out."*

*"Would you be proud to put that in front of our customer?"*

This chain-smoking chef was the epitome of the Japanese concept of *Shokunin*. In the 2011 documentary *Jiro Dreams of Sushi*, the titular character uses this term to describe himself as someone who dedicates completely to bettering his craft. He was obligated on an almost spiritual level to constant improvement. Regardless of how exhausted he was, or the financial state of the restaurant, the inventory, or any other externality, he would never compromise on quality.

At the time, I had already given up on my ambitions of becoming a chef. I was enrolled in university, pursuing a degree in civil engineering. I took on a few shifts to make ends meet and aimed to exert as little effort as possible to earn some money. Regardless, Chef would not allow me to compromise in any way. During post-service debriefs, he regularly shared his motivating philosophy. While the staff spent half our lives in that kitchen, pushing out endless plates of food to people we would never see, on the other side of that exchange was a human being. We were not just feeding them; we were providing an experience.

His sense of empathy, which he somehow retained after thirty years in high-pressure kitchens, is inspiring in hindsight, but was absolutely infuriating in the moment. It is only after nearly twenty years, and now in a completely different industry, that I can finally appreciate his position. When immersed in a transformation initiative, it's tempting to view it as just one of many ongoing activities. We might cut corners, eager to move on to the next task. Yet, we must always remember that on the other side of that transaction are people who might only experience a few such initiatives in their entire career. Each project demands the same care and attention to detail. We cannot forget the radicchio.

This book has been organized to begin with an inward focus, turning outward in the second half. This partition is intended to mirror the personal development of a practitioner and the path of their career. After dedicating time to execution, we undergo an examination into the deeper meaning of value after becoming leaders.

The initial part of this book delves into incorporating empathy into the daily work of an individual, positioning it as a tool to achieve goals. For an individual contributor seeking to maximize their impact and advance in their career, an intentional focus on building empathy alongside technical skills can be a key differentiator. Amidst cubicles filled with mechanical keyboards and derisive laughs, a warm and understanding person will always be the first choice of stakeholders and leaders in need of support.

However, we soon come to the realization that implementation is the lowest value activity in the marketplace. Regardless of how empathetic or technically proficient a geek may be, their career and potential are capped by their own biology – they cannot exceed the output of a single person. The next step in their career is when they are in a position to manage other geeks.

In the second part of the book, we discussed embedding empathy into the technology practice. This involves understanding how to soften those angry keyboards and replace derision with sympathy, and to establish conventions that are conducive to building a high-performance team focused on value creation rather than technology. These human-centered technology functions, closely integrated with the business, can have a significant positive impact on their organizations. The barriers that exist for a purely technical practice come down over time when we have an intentional focus on empathy and relationship building. As managers, we can influence our teams towards this end.

Yet, the practice of team management does not represent the highest value in the marketplace. Regardless of how productive a team may be or how integrated they are with the rest of the organization, managers will play someone else's tune and be focused on implementation and execution, albeit with more horsepower and some tangential cultural impacts. The ultimate career stage, and the pinnacle of value, lies is in communication, having and exerting influence within our organizations.

Early-career practitioners are told, implicitly or explicitly, that they are seen as interchangeable. The stakeholder has an idea, and they just need somebody to execute it. In later years, as we reach management, we are reminded that our role is to guide the execution. When we reach more senior roles, we are expected to act as translators between business stakeholders and technical managers. In all but the most progressive organizations, we follow the standard career progression and remain order takers, simply taking orders from more senior leaders.

The reasons behind this paradigm are many, with fault lying on both sides. However, if we and our organizations are to be at our best, we cannot continue to be isolated from our stakeholders. The etymology of the word "company" is fascinating, tracing back to the 12$^{th}$ century Old French word *compagnie*, meaning society or friendship. Its negative connotations emerged only recently. Organizations are simply groups of people united in a common purpose; they are a community. As a community, we all need to be working together for the betterment of all.

Early social contract theorists had a lot to say about how community arose naturally. Hobbes believed we gathered to stave off fear and competition. Rosseau said that we are inherently solitary and fearful. All these foundational theories were based on the presupposition that people are naturally individualistic, suggesting that we only come together out of necessity. Our current understanding of anthropology contradicts this assumption. Throughout history, humans have never existed as isolated units as these theorists assumed.[172] Humans have evolved for community and need to be oriented towards a group to be satisfied.

---

[172] For an excellent summary of social contract theorists see Fukuyama, Francis. The Origins of Political Order: From Prehuman Times to the French Revolution. Farrar, Straus and Giroux, 2012.

This book was written to help elevate the technology practice by elevating the practitioners. Nobody cares about the code or technology, only what it can do for them. We cannot promote ourselves or our work on technical merit. We need to adapt to the business world to be successful and to focus our efforts on the creation of value.

Technology workers make their mark in helping others, and to help others we need to begin with empathy. Understanding deeply and personally what the motivations, constraints, ambitions, and emotional posture are of the other person.

It is my hope that readers will come to see empathy as both a personal characteristic that leads to greater success and mental health, as well as a business asset to be cultivated within the technology function. Human factors will be a key differentiator for future practitioners, and geeks with empathy are going to be the change-makers in their organizations.

# EPILOGUE

In an attempt to maintain the narrative flow of the book, some topics were discussed only briefly that warrant a more in-depth exploration. It is important to examine current trends specific to several technology functions and roles to articulate a specific case for change.

## The Future of the CIxO Role

During the initial interaction with a chief technology executive, a practitioner is likely to be struck by their uncharacteristic assertiveness. The technology practice is rife with paper tigers, but encountering an individual who combines genuine conviction with executive presence is rare. If this personality type is found in someone with the technical breadth to understand their stack and the industry knowledge to interface with their peers, they naturally gravitate towards executive roles. Unfortunately, the critical factor in their success is usually their similarity to executive colleagues rather than their ability to guide their reports. With equally uncharacteristic political acumen, they tend to prioritize relationships over results.

The level below, encompassing vice presidents and directors, often has the opposite weighting. Well-established in their field, they possess a genuine ability to connect with their reports. They can reframe cascading strategic goals and direct their team to execute. However, their personal focus on technology and resource management often leaves them unable to articulate a compelling vision that can excite senior executives. Pressed against a career ceiling for years, they wait and hope, while their leaders, eventually losing the confidence of their executive peers, churn between the few available executive seats in the market, bringing new and exciting ideas for their downtrodden reports to implement.

This cycling of short-tenured technology executives is particularly apparent with chief data officer roles. In a study by Cindi Howson and Sonny Rivera they found that one quarter of CDOs were still in their first year on the job, and that the primary focus of these defensive CDOs was to safeguard data and institute tight data governance policies.[173]

The second generation of CDOs, brought on to loosen the reins, were much more focused on improving business operations, value creation, and monetization. As organizations improve in their data literacy, and as executive leadership teams gain experience with these leaders, they come to realize that a mature technology leader is not simply an angrier practitioner, but one who can direct technology to improve the bottom line. This evolution mirrors the historical shift of the CFO role, which initially focused on managing finances but eventually came to drive business results.

What we also come to realize through this slow maturation of technology leadership is that practitioners have unique

---

[173] ThoughtSpot, "9 data and analytics trends for 2023", 2022.

needs to be at their best. Tailoring management styles and performance evaluation to suit different roles within technology, be it IT delivery, data science, or business advisory, can significantly enhance retention rates, engagement levels, and overall profitability. Adjusting leadership approaches to accommodate the diverse requirements of these roles acknowledges their distinct contributions and fosters a more supportive and performant work environment.

Less mature executive leaders try to build credibility with fellow executives with the promise of controlling an enigmatic function with quantitative productivity targets. They point to increased story points delivered per sprint or lines of code per week as evidence of their success. However, as organizations evolve, leaders come to the realization that these metrics alone do not translate into real business results. This understanding prompts a shift in leadership priorities, encouraging a more nuanced and outcome-oriented approach in subsequent leaders.

In a 2019 Gallup study conducted in the United States, it was revealed that only 4 out of 10 employees believe that their leaders genuinely care for them as individuals.[174] Positive personal relationships are identified as one of the most crucial factors in fostering engagement, yet there tends to be an assumption that technology workers are immune to this need. In reality, many technology workers may still feel unappreciated or uncared for, even if they are less likely to express these sentiments compared to individuals in other functions. Instead of authentic care, organizations often resort to offering infantilizing perks like foosball tables and espresso machines.

The end goal of technology is to help people work more effectively. This holds true for both digital native companies

---

[174] Gallup. "State of the American Workplace." Gallup, 2019.

and legacy companies. Consequently, conversations around technology stack and architectural preferences will eventually shift towards emphasizing human factors and change management. Organizations that prioritize transparent and easily maintainable solutions will have a strategic advantage over those simply adopt the latest technology trends, assuming that value will naturally follow.

The CIxO roles of the future will be held by leaders who can confidently switch hats between results-driven Napoleons and human-centric Nightingales. Non-technical executives, as they come to view technology as an enabler, will likewise come to understand the importance of seasoned leaders who can work in the grey. It will be those who collaborate that are most successful in reaching the highest levels of their organizations. Empathizing with their peers by translating technology into business terms. Empathizing with their customers by implementing easy to use solutions. Empathizing with their employees by building a healthy working environment. Without a focus on empathy and an understanding of their stakeholders at all levels, the intractable CIxOs of today will find themselves independent consultants.

## Future of AI, Analytics, and Data Science

AI practitioners, as descendants of operations research and decision support, were some of the first to be closely integrated into the business. Over time, they became more divorced from daily operations as the practice became more proceduralized. Early in their history, their work may have used statistics to support resource management and required field work to gather data. These types of operational improvements are now more likely to be performed in a separate office using existing data, and providing recommendations that impact front line workers who the geeks will never meet. They continue to add value to the organization by augmenting or automating decision-making, but they are highly dependent on unfamiliar data.

Charles Babbage, a patriarch of computing, was one of the first to see "work" as a system and attempted to use data to monitor and control it to improve efficiency.[175] Babbage believed that the factory itself was perfect, and that human failure and inconsistency were the only weak points in the system.[176] His view was that if we could deconstruct every piece of work into minute processes, we could optimize it to perfection. The goal was to eliminate the randomness introduced by individual ad hoc decisions, resulting in the most productive system possible.

That line of thinking has permeated the data and analytics space, contributing to a misanthropic culture. We see data in isolation, forgetting that each row in our data set represents human activity. We have often claimed that our efforts towards automated decision making will free people from repetitive tasks so they can focus on more value-added activities, but we, like Babbage, are quite pleased to have that randomness removed from our systems. Now, a decade into the professionalization of data science, most senior organizations are finding diminishing marginal benefit from ongoing investment using existing approaches.

When we moved originally from instincts and heuristics to data-driven decision making, analytics provided significant

---

[175] Babbage, Charles. On the Economy of Machinery and Manufacturing. Cambridge University Press, 2010. Originally published in 1832.
[176] Schaffer, S. (1994). Babbage's Intelligence: Calculating Engines and the Factory System. Critical Inquiry, 21(1), 203–227.

value. However, as we progressed, the ongoing benefit of having machine learning engineers fine-tune existing models decreased. The marginal benefit of adjusting our parameters on an operationalized model or swapping in a more effective algorithm is negligible in comparison to that original win.

With the low-hanging fruit picked, the alternatives are to shake the tree in the hopes of finding more opportunity, or to find the hidden trees. We will never know as much about the business as our colleagues, and it is only through partnership that we can find those new opportunities. The organizations that get the most benefit from their investment in data and analytics will be those that have them closely integrated with people in the business.

Empathy and collaboration are equally critical for professional development. In *Rule of the Robots*, author Martin Ford writes that AutoML and low-code solutions are lowering the barriers to entry for AI through democratization, and that the off-the-shelf availability of sophisticated tools from cloud providers will lead to a Cambrian explosion of new applications. He predicts that successful practitioners in the future will need to rely on their people skills and not their technical proficiency.[177]

In the two years between the publication of Ford's book and the authoring of this one, we have seen his predicted surge in the number of available tools realized. While each is designed to be self-sufficient, the narrow scope of each has required a sophisticated network of packages and tools to integrate. The presentation layer is more simplified than in past

---

[177] Ford, Martin. Rule of the Robots: How Artificial Intelligence Will Transform Everything. Basic Books, 2021.

years, but the supporting framework has exploded in complexity. This has led to a situation where data and analytics practitioners must either be savants with a broad toolkit or be highly collaborative.

With the recent surge in interest surrounding generative AI, each cloud provider is now developing their own ecosystem and toolset. Each of these tools will in the end have their own fan base, and the AI landscape will become even more fractured. The few gurus who have until now been able to rely on their immense technical talent will be culled further as they need to collaborate and depend on each other implicitly.

For the first part of its history, the driver of progress in AI has been scaling – leveraging more data and more complex neural networks. Geoff Hinton, a renowned expert in the field, once said, "you just need to keep making it bigger and faster and it will get better. There's no looking back now."[178] We are now hitting a peak with what can be accomplished using brute force. According to OpenAI, the resources needed for AI are doubling every 3.4 months.[179] The costs associated with AI are not just financial; researchers at the University of Massachusetts found a large deep learning project can emit as much $CO_2$ as five cars.[180]

People are realizing that it is not just an issue of integration, but that the cultural change that goes alongside a data transformation is perhaps the most challenging aspect. Surveying by Randy Bean shows that only 27% of organizations consider

---

[178] Markoff, John. "Scientists see promise in deep learning programs." New York Times, November 24, 2012.
[179] Amodei, Dario, and Danny Hernandez. "AI and Compute." OpenAI, 2018.
[180] Martineau, Kim. "Shrinking deep learning's carbon footprint" MIT Quest for Intelligence, August 7, 2020.

themselves as "data driven". Those organizations may have a data and analytics practice, but it exists in isolation and has a limited impact on the business. Practitioners need to attach critical thinking to their algorithms and to be intentional about relationship building to be successful.[181]

We need to understand the importance of humans in analytics and to share this with business leaders and customers. We can intuitively understand that the sunrise causes the rooster to crow and not vice versa, but the most powerful deep learning algorithm will never understand that. You cannot determine causation through purely computational analysis.[182] No matter how advanced our algorithms get, we will need humans to be involved.

### Future of Data Literacy

Twenty thousand years ago, sitting at a headwater of the Nile River in what is now the Democratic Republic of Congo, somebody used a piece of quartz to scrape notches into a bone the size of a pencil. Whatever this person was counting, they wanted to preserve a record of it. That bone, now known as the Ishango bone, is the earliest recorded piece of data that we have discovered. In South America, people stored data by tying knots into strings. In Mesopotamia, people made indentations into small pieces of clay using cut reeds. We pressed a summary of human art and history into golden discs and sent them into space. We store our commercial transactions by adjusting the

[181] Bean, Randy. "Why Becoming a Data-Driven Organization Is So Hard." Harvard Business Review, February 2022.
[182] Ford, Martin. Architects of Intelligence: The truth about AI from the people building it. Packt Publishing, 2018.

electromagnetic fields of solid-state drives, dispersed through-out the world in vast data centers. It seems that we are biolog-ically compelled to hoard data. Unfortunately, few of us use it effectively.

In a sobering survey by Qlik, it was found that only 11% of employees are confident in their ability to use data, despite 89% of executives expecting that they use it to defend their decisions.[183] We gather data to give us a sense of control, but we rarely use it in our decision making.

Every geek has had the experience of working with some-body who prides themselves on their intuition. Aided by sur-vivorship bias, they have experienced great success without the need for data, and they advocate the same behavior for others. Fortunately, this is becoming much less common as Gen X and millennials assume leadership roles. As baby boomers re-tire over the next decade, workplaces will be populated by peo-ple who have never known life without a computer.

For a technology practitioner this sounds like great news, but the danger is that we are replacing the intuition born of a lifetime of experience with the blind acceptance of data as fact. Data literacy, taken to the extreme, is far worse than gut feel. Decisions made based on intuition leaves room for negotia-tion, but confident action justified with incorrect data does not leave room for compromise.

Data literacy must be paired with careful deliberation to be effective. Understanding the data, being able to contextualize it, and being able to facilitate dialogue among stakeholders, will lead to a new type of data literacy. It needs to be a partnership based on mutual trust and respect, enabled by data. It is only

---

[183] Qlik. "Data Literacy: The Upskilling Evolution" 2022.

collaboration that will lead to positive outcomes, and not blind obedience to our biased datasets.

## Future of Technology Education

When professors design curricula, they establish several learning objectives to fulfill university requirements. These objectives include disciplinary knowledge, basic cognitive skills (numeracy, reading, etc.), higher-order cognitive skills (critical thinking, problem-solving, etc.), and soft skills (grit, teamwork, communication, adaptability, etc.). The implicit assumption is that achieving the former objectives will naturally lead to the development of the latter, and that soft skills will emerge as students collaborate on problem-solving activities as a team.[184]

Meanwhile, employers consistently express concerns about the lack of soft skills in new graduates. In Canada, the Canadian Council of Chief Executives emphasized that the most crucial qualifications for new graduates are problem-solving, communication, and relationship-building skills, placing them ahead of even disciplinary knowledge.[185] They would rather hire empathetic pragmatists than skilled technologists or abstract thinkers. The World Economic Forum echoes these sentiments, highlighting that the key success factors globally are problem-solving, critical thinking, people management, creativity, and communication.[186]

---

[184] Weingarten, Harvey P. Nothing Less than Great: Reforming Canada's Universities. University of Toronto Press, 2021.
[185] Conference Board of Canada. "Employability Skills." 2022. See also Stirrett, Scott. "It's human skills – not technical skills – that we need the most in today's workforce." Globe and Mail, August 8, 2017.
[186] World Economic Forum. "The future of jobs employment,

This perspective conflicts with the traditional view of a liberal education, which is intended to "draw on Socrates' concept of 'the examined life', on Aristotle's notions of reflective citizenship, and above all on Greek and Roman Stoic notions of an education that is 'liberal' in that it liberates the mind from bondage of habit and custom, producing people who can function with sensitivity and alertness as citizens of the whole world."[187] There are few arguments for an ignorant citizenry, but it cannot come at the cost of employability or basic life skills. More students are pursuing STEM degrees for the prospect of a high-paying career and turning away from the humanities.[188] Universities, faced with declining enrolment in the arts, subsidize these waning programs by requiring STEM majors take courses in them as electives.

Taken in combination, many of today's graduates are entering the workforce with much of their education focused on the arts, pure sciences, and theoretical foundations. The problems that organizations face require managerial skills, communication, creativity, and foundational technical abilities. This misalignment places strain on employers who need to invest ever-more time to get new graduates ramped up.

Universities in the future will need to focus on experiential learning and lean heavily into partnerships with corporate sponsors. Collaborating with employers to understand their needs and build a curriculum not around a traditional liberal education, but on developing high-performing and empathetic

---

skills, and workforce strategy for the fourth industrial revolution." WEF, 2016.
[187] Nussbaum, Martha. Cultivating Humanity: A Classical Defense of Reform in Education. Harvard University Press, 1997.
[188] Schmidt, Benjamin. "The Humanities Are In Crisis." The Atlantic, 2018.

workers.

## Future of Technology Work

People have always bemoaned the younger generation, claiming that they have a diminished work ethic. In 1987, Sean Sayers wrote, "young people in particular, it appears, are becoming more demanding in relation to work: they are less willing to submit quietly to arbitrary authority, and they want fulfilment from their work. The idea that work of whatever kind is a duty and a virtue is passing – if, indeed, it was ever widespread."[189] In 1904, Granville Hall wrote, "Never has youth been exposed to such dangers [...] increasing urban life with its temptations, prematurities, sedentary occupations, and passive stimuli just when an active life is most needed, early emancipation and a lessening sense for both duty and discipline, the haste to know and do all befitting man's estate before its time."[190] This concern is documented as far back as 1695 when Robert Russel discussed towns full of lazy youth addressing each other by nicknames and other "filthy [c]ommunications"[191] rather than working.

Concerns around work ethic seem natural, but what is new for our younger generation is the urgency with which they are tuning out from work. Timothy Leary may have encouraged boomers to "turn on, tune in, and drop out", but his listeners became workaholics within a decade. The modern anti-work movement has a more fundamental concern – that no amount

---

[189] Sayers, Sean. "The Need to Work" Radical Philosophy, 1987.
[190] Hall, G. Stanley. The Psychology of Adolescence. New York: Appleton and Company, 1904.
[191] Russel, Robert. A Little Book for Children and Youth. Originally published 1695.

of effort can secure for them the lifestyle that their parents have.

Some sociologists celebrate the end of the Protestant work ethic and believe that people are waking up from the societally induced artificial compulsion to work.[192] Many believe a change in priorities will lead to greater personal satisfaction.

The 'future of work' industry is not a new phenomenon. Since the 1980s, prognosticators have tried to extrapolate trends. While they often get the form correct in the short term, the details tend to be grossly inaccurate. Gen Z, as they mature, might evolve into highly productive workers, leveraging their multitasking abilities to tackle challenges that prior generations would have struggled with. Their fragility and lack of competitive instinct may lead to new levels of collaboration.

One certainty, regardless of the details, is that building authentic human connections will be critical. Boomers and Gen X were adept at separating business from personal spheres and could handle criticism without permanent harm. They could also separate a colleague's personal life and beliefs from their working relationship. Neither is the case for the younger generations. Success in the future will demand adaptation to the needs of these new practitioners, both professionally and personally.

## Closing

Technology is often cited as one of the fastest-changing

---

[192] Gorz, André. Farewell to the Working Class: An Essay on Post-Industrial Socialism. Pluto Press, 1997.

fields. Without a clear focus on continuous education and personal development, practitioners can quickly find themselves falling behind their peers. However, the overarching social contract between our practices and the organizations we serve has not changed since the 1970s.

There is no doubt that organizations fully leveraging their technology function will gain a significant advantage over their competitors. Equally clear is that practitioners who can reorient themselves to a service mindset will experience greater happiness and success in their fields.

The specific form that this will take varies by country, culture, industry, organization, function, and field. While this epilogue has made efforts to explore specific areas, it cannot be exhaustive.

As a practice, we must adopt not a new operating framework or delivery methodology, but rather a new north star. We need to understand our role is not the simple deployment of new technologies, but the strategic leveraging of technology in the service of our colleagues and customers.

While the specific form will vary, there is one certainty: the intentional development of empathy will be a key differentiator for future practitioners, and geeks with empathy are going to be the change-makers in their organizations.

# ACKNOWLEDGEMENTS

I have had the good fortune to work for and with some of the most amazing people, and each one of them, in some way, influenced this work. Whether you were my colleague, champion, detractor, co-conspirator, leader, report, peer, student, teacher, client, vendor, or classmate, I learned something of great value from you that I have tried to capture here, and I thank you for it.

Over the two years that this book has been in development, I have had kind support of countless people.

I want to give a big thank you to my early reviewers who waded through the early drafts, providing essential guidance for the book's development: Renée Francis, the kindest person I know, Vardan Matevosyan, the most AWSome architect, and Chris Sorenson, single handedly bringing empathy to consulting. I also extend my appreciation to early proofreaders Malik Hassan, Dan Poon, and Wilco Van Ginkel.

Thank you as well to my amazing family who supported me through another book, Finley, Wyatt, Gideon, and Melodie.

A big shoutout to Farrukh Khan for designing the perfect cover.

Lastly, thank you to my readers and supporters. Your kind reviews and emails are what made *Minding the Machines* worthwhile and served as motivation for this work.

# ABOUT THE AUTHOR

Jeremy Adamson is a technology strategy leader with extensive experience working with clients in retail, transportation, energy, financial services, and the public sector. He has worked with several major organizations to help them establish a leadership position in data science and to unlock real business value using advanced analytics.

Jeremy holds a Master's degree in Transportation Engineering and a Bachelor's degree in Civil Engineering from the University of New Brunswick, as well as a Master of Business Administration from the University of Calgary. Jeremy lives and works between Alberta and the Maritimes in Canada.

Learn more at https://www.rjeremyadamson.com